Virginia Hill's
Learn to Microwave

Virginia Hill became a microwave demonstrator with the Sharp Corporation in 1977. She soon realised that there was a need for more consumer education on microwave cooking and established her own consultancy, the Microwave Cooking Centre, in 1980.

To reach a larger audience than she could through her classes, in 1982 she produced *The All Australian Microwave Recipe Book* and an accompanying video. She has since had a number of books published. Her *Microwave Tips and Techniques* was published by Penguin Books Australia in 1991 and reprints regularly. In 1992 she published *Virginia Hill's Microwave Companion* (Viking O'Neil), an encyclopaedia of microwave cooking, and *Microwave Stack Cooking* (Tupperware Australia Pty Ltd and Regency Publications Pty Ltd) and in 1993 her popular *Microwave Cooking for Babies and Toddlers* (Viking O'Neil) appeared.

In addition to her consultancy and classes, Virginia Hill writes an occasional column in the Melbourne *Age* and broadcasts weekly on radio 3AW.

Virginia Hill's
Learn to
Microwave

VIKING

Viking
Penguin Books Australia Ltd
487 Maroondah Highway, PO Box 257
Ringwood, Victoria 3134, Australia
Penguin Books Ltd
Harmondsworth, Middlesex, England
Viking Penguin, A Division of Penguin Books USA Inc.
375 Hudson Street, New York, New York 10014, USA
Penguin Books Canada Limited
10 Alcorn Avenue, Toronto, Ontario, Canada M4V 3B2
Penguin Books (N.Z.) Ltd
182–190 Wairau Road, Auckland 10, New Zealand

First published by Penguin Books Australia Ltd 1994

10 9 8 7 6 5 4 3 2 1

Typeset in 10½/12½ pt Palatino by Midland
Typesetters, Maryborough, Victoria
Design by Catherine Howarth
Food preparation (front cover) by Kay Cafarella
Printed in Australia by Australian Print Group,
Maryborough, Victoria

National Library of Australia
Cataloguing-in-Publication data

Hill, Virginia.
    Learn to microwave

    Includes index.
    ISBN 0 670 90688 3.

    1. Microwave cookery. I. Title.

641.5882

CONTENTS

Acknowledgements

My thanks to Kay Cafarella for recipe development assistance and to my editor, Clare Coney.

INTRODUCTION

The microwave oven has become a kitchen essential, yet many owners are unconfident when using their microwave ovens and hesitant to experiment with their special features and finer points.

To master the microwave use the oven every day. You will find with practice that the microwave will cook about 75 per cent of foods. Use it for what it does best and the microwave will produce excellent results while saving time and money.

Microwave cooking is so fast that you will change many of your traditional meal-planning steps. First review the menu. Work out which dishes are best made in the microwave oven, and then determine the best order for cooking them. Start by cooking the food with the longest standing time (see page 7) and then cook in sequence to the shortest standing time. For instance, begin with a cake or dessert, which may be served warm or cold, then cook the main dish, followed by potatoes, a green vegetable and gravy or sauce.

Many dishes continue to cook when they are removed from the microwave oven. This carry-over cooking occurs during the standing time and it also means the heat transferred from the outside to the centre keeps most food warm, until serving, if covered. If food does cool, remember it quickly reheats in the microwave at serving time.

Although you may have bought the oven primarily for its cooking speed and convenience, you can vary the power you cook with for different types of food (as you would vary the temperature when cooking conventionally) to produce the results you are accustomed to. You will therefore see some recipes using less than HIGH power, when it is appropriate.

Relate your microwave cooking techniques to conventional cooking by asking yourself what you want to happen to the food – a baked/dry finish, a steamed/moist finish, a casserole/slow cook or a stir fry/ crunchy finish? To achieve these in the microwave, various cooking techniques are used, just as in conventional cooking. Food is covered to steam, elevated on a rack to bake, or roasted semi-covered with baking paper or paper towel to prevent spatters and create a dry roast finish.

Microwave cooking differs from conventional because you time the cooking according to the weight of the food, rather than adjust the temperature. Correct timing is vital, and a set of kitchen scales, in conjunction with the time charts in this book, will be your most important microwave accessory. Check the cookware section of the book (pages 8–10) for commonsense utensils and other useful microwave accessories to help make your job easier – I have only recommended items that you really need for good cooking results.

In the beginning, try a few easy recipes and add to these as you become more confident. There is nothing like success to dispel the fear of using your microwave oven. Remember that the microwave cooks food in about a third of the time of conventional cooking. You will also find that your kitchen stays much cooler!

The simplicity of this book will make your microwave cooking fun, not work, so use your microwave every day and for every meal.

Recipes in this book have been developed for 600–800 watt microwave ovens. Check the wattage of your oven and add 10 per cent extra to the cooking time if yours is 500 watts.

HOW MICROWAVE OVENS WORK

Microwaves are high-frequency, short-length electromagnetic waves. The familiar domestic bench-top microwave oven consists of two metal boxes, one inside the other, and a door made of metal mesh sandwiched between high impact polypropylene. Because microwaves cannot penetrate metal, they bounce off the oven's walls. They can pass through microwave cookware containers and thus penetrate into the food from all directions, up to a depth of 4 cm.

When a microwave oven is turned on, the microwaves are made from everyday household electricity inside a tube called a magnetron, the heart of the oven. These waves are directed into the oven cavity by a wave guide positioned either at the top or side of the oven.

Once the microwaves are absorbed into food they simply vibrate its water, fat and sugar molecules 2½ billion times per second to create friction and instant heat inside the food. That is why microwave cooking is so fast. The centre of food (anything more than 4 cm from its surface) is cooked by the conduction of heat, as in conventional cooking.

Once the oven is turned off or the door opened, the microwaves cease to be generated and there is no residue left in the cooked food, which is merely hot.

MICROWAVE OVEN SAFETY

In Australia, microwave ovens are subject to stringent safety standards, and a seal around the oven door ensures the microwaves are contained inside the oven. There is no possible way that microwaves can be present once the oven door is opened, as a special system ensures that the slightest movement to the door catch stops their generation.

The microwave oven is one of the safest kitchen appliances if used as intended. There are two simple rules. First, do not turn the oven on whilst empty or you will damage it. Leave a jug of water in the microwave oven when it is not in use so if it is inadvertently turned on the water will attract the microwaves and prevent damage to the oven's magnetron. Second, do not put any metal objects in the microwave, except aluminium foil (see page 10).

If you are concerned about your oven, have it checked out by a qualified technician.

OVEN CLEANING

Microwave ovens are easy to clean as they do not heat up, so spatters and spills do not bake on as they do in conventional ovens. If possible, wipe your oven out whilst it is still warm as fatty spots left on the ceiling or oven walls tend to absorb microwave energy during cooking. Wiping the inside of the microwave oven after every use is the easiest and quickest way of keeping the oven clean.

Depending on the food you are cooking, you will find from time to time that moisture forms on the door and walls of the unit. Steam emanating from foods is quite normal and can be easily wiped away at the end of cooking time.

Day-to-day cleaning should be done as soon as practicable after using the oven. Dampen several sheets of top-quality, non-recycled plain paper towel with warm water, squeeze and place in the microwave oven. Heat on HIGH power (90–100%) for 20–25 seconds. This will create a steamy interior and warm the paper cloth, so that you can wipe the oven cavity clean. Make sure the area around the door seal is kept thoroughly clean of food and splatters. Dry the oven cavity with clean sheets of paper towel.

Stubborn food stains are best removed by boiling some water in the oven for 5–10 minutes, and then wiping over the areas of cooked-on food with a soft pad.

Should you need to deodorise the oven after cooking fish or broccoli, bring a cup of water with 2 lemon slices in it to the boil on HIGH (90–100%) for 2–3 minutes, then wipe the inside cavity and leave the door open for a few hours.

THE BASICS OF MICROWAVE COOKING

1 THINK MICROWAVE First, you need to *'think microwave'* when using the microwave oven, just as you now automatically *'think conventional'*. Ask yourself what you are aiming to do and which technique will best achieve it. Decide if the cooking needs a power other than HIGH. Select the right cooking container for, as with conventional cooking, the size of the container should relate to the amount of food being cooked.

   With increasing microwave experience, these decisions will become automatic over time.

2 WATTAGE As basic as this sounds, it is important that you know the wattage of your own oven so you know the exact amount of microwave power you have available for cooking. Oven wattages now range from 500 through to 900 watts. The recipes in this book have been developed for 600–800 watt ovens. If you are using a 500-watt unit, you will need to add 10 per cent extra to the cooking time in the recipes.

3 MICROWAVE POWER SETTINGS Your oven may have two, five or ten power settings. Most modern microwaves provide five preset power levels. These variable power levels allow you to adjust the cooking power, to get better and more even results, just as a conventional oven has adjustable temperatures to suit different kinds of foods and cooking methods. Variable power levels work by cycling on and off at intervals to produce different percentages of HIGH (FULL) power, so that your cooking may be slowed down to suit the recipe.

All modern microwave ovens have a DEFROST setting which can also be used for gentle or slow cooking.

4 TIMING Cooking time depends on weight. It's most important to know *exactly* how much food you are microwaving or defrosting. Weigh your oven-ready food, then refer to the relevant, handy cooking chart in this book. Cooking is also affected by size, shape, density, composition and starting temperature of food – see numbers 5–9 below.

5 SIZE Large pieces of food take longer to cook than smaller, slender foods. This is because small food quantities receive almost total microwave penetration, whereas larger quantities (especially meat roasts) complete their cooking by the conduction of the heat produced by the microwaves from the outer areas to the centre.

6 SHAPE Evenly shaped foods cook best in the microwave oven, as with uneven food the thin areas cook more rapidly than the thicker portions. For instance, the shank end of a leg of lamb cooks faster than the rest of the meat, so boned and uniform shaped meat is recommended. Otherwise you need to shield the slimmer areas of food with small, smooth pieces of aluminium foil to keep them from over-exposure to the microwave energy. The foil reflects microwaves and slows the cooking.

7 DENSITY AND FOOD FIBRES Foods of similar sizes but different densities and textures will cook at different rates. If a potato and tomato are the same size, the tomato will cook faster because it is softer. Likewise, if a meatloaf and roast are the same size, the meatloaf will cook more quickly because it is less dense.

8 FOOD COMPOSITION Microwaves are attracted to fat, sugar and moisture – in that order. For this reason the speed of microwave cooking will vary depending upon the composition of the food being cooked. Bone content also affects the cooking. Certain recipes may therefore recommend removing the fat and bone from meat or poultry or stirring dishes thoroughly and eliminating salt, which dehydrates microwaved food.

9 STARTING TEMPERATURE This can make a big difference to the timing and cooking results of food. All recipes in this book assume food is at room temperature when put into the microwave oven.

10 QUANTITY Microwave cooking totally differs from conventional cooking in that cooking four fish fillets conventionally takes no more time than cooking two fillets, but when using the microwave oven the cooking time is almost doubled for four. This is because the amount of microwave energy absorbed by each fillet is reduced when the food quantity is increased. More food requires more time so, for accuracy, always weigh food then check with your microwave cooking chart to establish the correct timing.

11 ARRANGING FOOD Make sure you place the thicker portions of food to the outer edge of the dish or turntable. Microwaves travel from the outside to the centre of a dish, which heats more slowly than the edges. To cook multiple items, place foods that take longer to cook on the outer edge of the container, with quicker cooking foods in the centre. A circle or doughnut shape is the ideal cooking shape for microwaves. Leave some space between the food pieces if possible, as this allows microwaves to penetrate quickly and evenly.

12 COOKWARE The right containers make a difference to microwave timing and cooking results. Where possible use microware: this is made of quality durable plastic, marked specifically 'Safe for microwave use'. Microwaves pass through it, leaving the container cool. Always select the right size container for the quantity of food being cooked, as specified in the recipe, or the timing and finished results may be different from your expectations.

     You can also use ovenproof glass, pyro-ceramics, porcelain and china, or stoneware and pottery that is well glazed. If cooking in these dishes, you need to be aware that the cooking times for recipes will require 5–7 minutes longer per 500 g food as these types of cookware materials prolong microwave cooking times. You **must not** put metal in the microwave; this includes gold decoration on plates.

13 STANDING TIME This is an important part of overall microwave cooking. It is used to complete the cooking process, as some cooking will automatically continue within the food after the oven is turned off. This is because the heat within the food will continue to transfer while the food rests prior to serving. There is no way to stop this, so microwave cooking times are calculated to include standing time in the recipe's total cooking time. **Standing time is usually about one-quarter of the overall cooking time.** Always allow the food to stand, covered, as directed in the recipes. Standing time is sometimes called carry-over or ongoing cooking.

PRACTICAL
MICROWAVE UTENSILS
••

The right utensils are important in ensuring successful and fast micro-wave cooking results.

ESSENTIAL
- Set of accurate scales.
- Microware – specially designed strong plastic containers that give the fastest, most even and effective cooking results. The following are useful day-to-day microware containers.

Small container	400 ml (1⅔ cup)
Medium container	1 litre (4 cup)
Large container	1.5 litre (6 cup)
Extra-large container	2.25 litre (9 cup)

The size of the cooking container makes a difference to the cooking results and should always relate to the amount of food being cooked.

OTHER USEFUL PIECES
- 500 ml (2 cup) ovenable glass jug
- 1 litre (4 cup) ovenable glass jug
- Spoonwhisk (combines one tablespoon measure with a whisk)
- Roasting rack
- Cake ring dish
- Blender
- Sieve

MATCHING COOKWARE TO RECIPE

● Overfilling containers results in spills and uneven cooking.
● A dish too large for the amount of food being cooked may cause over cooking at the edges and leave an uncooked centre.
● Deeper dishes are good for soups and sauces that need stirring to equalise the temperature.
● Round containers with straight sides are best as they receive an even distribution of microwave energy. Square containers accumulate microwaves in the corners and cause uneven cooking.
● If you are not sure whether a dish is suitable for the microwave, put the empty dish with a glass measuring cup half filled with water in the oven and set it on HIGH (90–100%) for 1 minute. At the end of that time if the water is hot and the dish remains cool, the container is safe to use.

ACCESSORIES

Some accessories have been mentioned throughout this book. These are generally used for covering food in the microwave oven so it cooks properly.

PLASTIC WRAP AND LIDS
Food often has to be tightly covered when microwaving. Use microwave-safe plastic wrap (this will be printed on the packet) or a lid made of microwave-safe material so moisture is retained in the dish. The cooking time will be faster and steam helps to ensure food is tender, especially vegetables, casseroles and meat such as silverside, so these foods are always cooked covered.

ABSORBENT WHITE NON-RECYCLED PAPER TOWELS
These may be used to cover meat to give a dry finish and prevent spattering. Paper towels are also useful covers for foods that require frequent stirring, such as custard and savoury sauces. Paper towels are used to line cake rings to absorb excess moisture as they can easily be peeled off the bottom of the cake after standing time. Paper towels are also recommended as a cover when a dry finish is required for a microwave-baked cake.

BAKING PAPER
This is useful to hold in some steam and prevent spatters when

cooking foods such as fish that do not need much steam to keep them moist.

OVEN BAGS

These are good for cooking less tender cuts of meat. They can also be used to reheat leftovers successfully and to steam fibrous foods such as green beans. Secure these bags with a rubber band, string, or a tie of plastic cut from the top of the bag. Ties with metal wires through must not be used.

ALUMINIUM FOIL

Contrary to popular myth, small quantities of smooth aluminium foil can be used in the microwave oven. Make sure you have at least 70 per cent food to 30 per cent foil covering, and never completely cover food. Ensure that no foil touches the interior oven walls as this will cause arcing (sparking) and can damage the microwave.

Use smooth foil to shield small areas of foods such as chicken wings or fish tails to prevent them overcooking. Shallow foil containers used for commercially frozen convenience food may also be put in the microwave; their foil-coated lids should be removed. If necessary cover the food with microwave-safe plastic wrap or plain paper towel.

Weigh oven-ready food so you can work out the correct cooking or defrosting time from the charts.

DEFROSTING

One of the major advantages of the microwave oven is the defrost function which enables you to thaw food quickly without any flavour loss. Not only is this a benefit to working cooks or families with uncoordinated mealtime schedules, but it also means there is little wastage of unused food, as it can be frozen and defrosted on another occasion.

How you prepare and wrap food for freezing helps you to defrost it quickly and well. Weigh and pack food in smallish quantities – 0.5–1 kg where possible – ensuring the packages are evenly shaped and labelled, as the defrosting time will vary with the frozen temperature of the food, its shape and the wattage of your oven. Large quantities of food, such as roasts or cooked dishes, should be elevated on a roasting rack or saucer for more even defrosting results.

The defrost power allows food to thaw at 30 per cent of the total microwave power output. Microwaves are thus active for 30 per cent of the time only and the remainder is resting time. This ensures that the ice crystals melt slowly and helps prevent the food from cooking.

FOR DEFROSTING SUCCESS

- Allow the minimum defrosting time recommended. Excess heat ruins food, and extra time can always be added if it is required. The best result is achieved if the food is still slightly icy at standing time and is then allowed to thaw naturally.
- Take special care to defrost poultry thoroughly as it must be totally thawed before cooking. Chicken should be turned half-way through

the defrosting time and thick pieces separated. Always rinse thawed poultry in cold water and let stand for 5–10 minutes at room temperature before cooking. Cook poultry immediately, or refrigerate, after defrosting.

● Turn foods over at least once during defrosting.
● Pierce microwave-safe plastic wraps, pouches, skins or membranes before thawing.
● Break up blocks of frozen food with a fork during defrosting time so the frozen parts are brought to the edges.
● Separate foods such as sausages, chops and hamburgers as they defrost, to prevent cooking.
● Remove drips and juice from frozen food as it thaws because moisture continues to attract microwaves and slows the defrosting process.
● Remember standing time at the end of defrosting time, when the heat produced within the food will continue the thawing process by conduction. Standing time after defrosting is generally longer than after other microwave cooking.
● Shield areas that are thawing too fast, or becoming warm, with small pieces of smooth foil. Remember that no metal should touch the walls of the oven.

DEFROSTING GUIDE

Begin by selecting the minimum defrosting time. This will prevent overheating and more time can always be added at the end if the defrosting is not complete.

FOOD	TECHNIQUE	POWER	TIME
BREAD Pita	Leave in plastic packet wrapping for first 2 min. then separate slices and spread over paper towel to prevent sogginess. Do not stand pita bread as it goes hard.	DEFROST (30–35%)	6 slices: 2–3 min.

FOOD	TECHNIQUE	POWER	TIME
Roll	Place on paper towel. Time very carefully. Check to ensure rolls do not overheat. Do not stand as rolls may go hard.	HIGH (90–100%)	1 roll: 15–20 sec. 2 rolls: 30–45 sec. 3 rolls: 1–1½ min.
Slice	Place between paper towel. Do not stand.	HIGH (90–100%)	15 sec.
Whole sliced loaf	Defrost in plastic packet wrapping. Remove metal tags. Let stand in packet wrapping.	HIGH (90–100%)	1 small: 2–4 min. + 10 min. standing time. 1 large: 4–6 min. + 10 min. standing time.
Whole unsliced loaf	Remove from plastic packet wrapping. Turn over half-way through defrosting. Stand on paper towel.	MEDIUM (50–60%)	1 small: 2–4 min. + 10 min. standing time. 1 large: 4–5 min. + 10 min. standing time.
CAKE Fruit (about 750 g)	Elevate on roasting rack. Cover loosely with paper towel. Stand half-way through defrosting. The dense texture requires slow defrosting.	DEFROST (30–35%)	2–3 min. defrost then stand 2–3 min. Another 2–3 min. defrost + 10 min. standing time.
Patty	Place paper towel on roasting rack. Elevate cakes on outer edge of rack. Loosely cover with paper towel. Time very carefully. Check to ensure patty cakes do not overheat.	MEDIUM (50–60%)	2 cakes: 30–60 sec. + 5 min. standing time. 4 cakes: 1–1½ min. + 5 min. standing time.
Sponge and cream	Cover roasting rack with paper towel. Stand cake on rack and loosely cover with paper towel. Time very carefully – ensure cake does not overheat.	DEFROST (30–35%)	1–1½ min. in 10 sec. bursts + 20–30 min. standing time.

FOOD	TECHNIQUE	POWER	TIME
CROIS-SANTS	Place on paper towel.	HIGH (90–100%)	1–2 croissants: 10–20 sec. in 10 sec. bursts + 1–2 min. standing time. 4 croissants: 1–1½ min. in 10 sec. bursts + 2–3 min. standing time.
DOUGH-NUTS, JAM	Place on paper towel. Standing time is extremely important, as jam in centre can be very hot.	MEDIUM (50–60%)	2 doughnuts: 45–60 sec. + 2–5 min. standing time. 4 doughnuts: 45–90 sec. + 2–5 min. standing time.
FISH AND SEAFOOD Cutlet (flake, gemfish, John Dory)	Place on roasting rack. Shield thin ends with foil. Stand for 5 minutes about half-way through defrosting. Pat dry before cooking.	DEFROST (30–35%)	per 500 g: 3 min + 5 min. standing time. Another 2–3 min. + 10 min. standing time.
Fingers	Place on roasting rack. If necessary defrost further on HIGH (90–100%) for 1 more min.	DEFROST (30–35%)	6 fingers: 3–4 min. + 4 min. standing time.
Prawns, commercial frozen	Remove from packet and place on roasting rack. Loosely cover with paper towel. After standing stir well with fork and rinse well under running water.	DEFROST (30–35%)	100 g packet: 2–3 min. + 2 min. standing time.
Seafood, shelled and loose (crabmeat, mussels, prawns)	Place on roasting rack. Loosely cover with paper towel. Stand for 5 min. between defrosts, then stand for 10 min. before cooking.	DEFROST (30–35%)	per 500 g: 2–3 min. then 5 min. standing time. Another 2–3 min. + 10 min. standing time.

FOOD	TECHNIQUE	POWER	TIME
Seafood, solid piece (crab)	Place in shallow dish. Cover with plastic wrap. Stand for 5 min. between defrosts, then stand for 10 min.	DEFROST (30–35%)	per 225 g: 2 min. then 5 min. standing time. Another 2 min. + 10 min. standing time.
Smoked salmon	Place on ovenable glass pie plate. Loosely cover with plastic wrap. Turn after 1 minute of defrosting. Leave to stand in refrigerator until completely defrosted.	DEFROST (30–35%)	per 200 g: 2–3 min. + standing time.
Steak (salmon, kingfish trevally)	Place thin end towards centre of roasting rack. Loosely cover with paper towel. Turn and stand for 2 min. half-way through defrosting. Separate large portions. Pat dry before cooking.	DEFROST (30–35%)	per 500 g: 3–4 min. + 2 min. standing time. Another 3–4 min. + 10 min. standing time.
Whole, large, gutted	Place on roasting rack. Shield thin ends with foil. Loosely cover with plastic wrap. Stand after first defrost, then turn over for second defrost. Pat dry before cooking.	DEFROST (30–35%)	per 1 kg: 8–10 min. then 20 min. standing time. Another 5 min. + 20–30 min. standing time.
Whole, small, gutted	Place in shallow dish. Loosely cover with paper towel. Turn during defrosting. Pat dry before cooking.	DEFROST (30–35%)	per 250 g: 5 min. + 10–15 min. standing time.
FLAN, FILLED	Stand on paper towel set on glass serving dish. Elevate on roasting rack. Remove paper towel before serving.	DEFROST (30–35%)	18-cm diameter: 4–5 min. + 5–10 min. standing time.
MEAT, COOKED Bolognese sauce	Shake and stir frequently during defrosting.	DEFROST (30–35%)	per 2 litres: 30 min. + 10 min. standing time.

FOOD	TECHNIQUE	POWER	TIME
Casserole	Stand half-way through defrosting.	DEFROST (30–35%)	per 750 g: 8–10 min. then 5 min. standing time. Another 8–10 min. + 15 min. standing time.
Plated meal	Do not overlap foods. Place thicker items towards edge of plate. Turn the plate around half-way through defrosting.	DEFROST (30–35%)	1 plate: 2–4 min. + 4 min. standing time.
MEAT, UN-COOKED Beef (joint, boned and rolled)	Elevate on roasting rack. Shield with foil as required, and turn during defrosting time.	DEFROST (30–35%)	per 500 g: 8–10 min. + 50 min. standing time.
Beef (joint, on the bone)	Elevate on roasting rack. Shield bone with foil, and turn regularly during defrosting time.	DEFROST (30–35%)	per 500 g: 9–10 min. +60 min. standing time.
Beef (steak, thick)	Elevate on roasting rack. Shield thin ends with foil and turn during defrosting time.	DEFROST (30–35%)	per 500 g: 6–9 min. + 10–12 min. standing time.
Cubed for casserole	Elevate on roasting rack. Separate and remove defrosted meat during defrosting time.	DEFROST (30–35%)	per 500 g: 8–10 min. + 10–15 min. standing time.
Lamb (chops)	Elevate on roasting rack. Separate during defrosting time.	DEFROST (30–35%)	per 500 g: 7–8 min. +5 min. standing time.
Lamb (leg)	Elevate on roasting rack. Shield narrow end with foil and turn during defrosting time.	DEFROST (30–35%)	per 500 g: 7–9 min. + 30–40 min. standing time.
Lamb (shoulder)	Elevate on roasting rack. Shield narrow end with foil and turn during defrosting time.	DEFROST (30–35%)	per 500 g: 6–8 min. + 30–40 min. standing time.

FOOD	TECHNIQUE	POWER	TIME
Mince	Elevate on roasting rack. Break up with fork and remove Defrosted meat during defrosting time.	DEFROST (30–35%)	per 500 g: 6–8 min. 10–15 min. standing time.
Offal (kidney and liver)	Elevate on roasting rack. Separate pieces during defrosting time.	DEFROST (30–35%)	per 500 g: 5–6 min. + 5 min. standing time.
Pork (chops)	Elevate on roasting rack. Separate during defrosting time.	DEFROST (30–35%)	per 500 g: 7–9 min. + 10 min. standing time.
Pork (joint)	Elevate on roasting rack. Shield fat and narrow ends with foil, and turn during defrosting time.	DEFROST (30–35%)	per 500 g: 7–8 min. + 50–60 min. standing time.
Sausages and sausage meat	Elevate on roasting rack. Separate and turn. Remove defrosted meat during defrosting time.	DEFROST (30–35%)	per 500 g: 5–6 min. + 8–10 min. standing time.
Veal (leg)	Elevate on roasting rack. Shield bone with foil,and turn during defrosting time.	DEFROST 30–35%)	per 500 g: 7–9 min. + 60–70 min. standing time.
Veal (shoulder)	Elevate on roasting rack. Shield bone with foil and turn during defrosting time.	DEFROST (30–35%)	per 500 g: 6–8 min. + 35–45 min. standing time.
PASTA Lasagne (home-made)	Stand half-way through defrosting.	DEFROST (30–35%)	Whole dish: 8–10 min. then 5 min. standing time. Another 8–10 min. +15 min. standing time.
Seafood	Place on glass serving dish. Loosely cover with plastic wrap. Break up half-way through defrosting with fork.	DEFROST (30–35%)	per 400 g: 7–8 min. + 5 min. standing time.

FOOD	TECHNIQUE	POWER	TIME
PASTRY Puff	Remove packet wrapping and stand on paper towel. Check frequently. Do not allow to get warm, or pastry will crack.	DEFROST (30–35%)	395 g packet: 2 min. + 20–30min. standing time.
Sausage rolls	Wrap each in paper towel to absorb moisture. Standing time is essential for best result.	DEFROST (30–35%)	4 large: 2½–3 min. + 5 min. standing time.
Shortcrust	Remove packet wrapping and stand on paper towel. Check frequently. Do not allow to get warm or pastry will crack.	DEFROST (30–35%)	225 g packet: 1 min. + 20 min. standing time.
POULTRY Chicken (pieces or joints)	Elevate on roasting rack. Separate pieces during defrosting time.	DEFROST (30–35%)	per 500 g: 7–10 min. + 10–15 min. standing time.
Chicken (whole)	Weigh to estimate correct time. Place breastside down on roasting rack, loosely covered, for first ⅓ of defrosting time. Turn bird over. Defrost another ⅓ time. Stand 5 minutes. Turn bird again and defrost remaining time. Ensure thorough defrosting. Wash well and dry before cooking.	DEFROST (30–35%)	per 500 g: 6–8 min. in 2–3 min. bursts, with 5 min. standing time after second defrost + 20–30 min. standing time at end.
Duck (whole)	As Chicken (whole).	DEFROST (30–35%)	per 500 g: 7 min. + 5 min. standing time after second defrost and 30 min. standing time at end.
Turkey (boned joint)	Elevate on roasting rack. Turn frequently.	DEFROST (30–35%)	per 500 g: 7–8 min. + 20–30 min. standing time.

FOOD	TECHNIQUE	POWER	TIME
Turkey (whole, 3.5–4 kg)	As Chicken (whole) but turn over three times.	DEFROST (30–35%)	per 500 g: 8–10 min. + 5 min. standing time half-way through defrosting + 50–60 min. standing time at end.
SOUP Home-made	Shake and stir frequently during defrosting. Add cream or yoghurt after defrosting.	HIGH (90–100%)	500 ml: 6–7 min. + 5 min. standing time. 1 litre: 15–16 min. + 8 min. standing time.
STOCK Home-made	Shake and stir frequently during defrosting.	HIGH (90–100%)	250 ml: 5 min. + 4 min. standing time. 500 ml: 8–10 min. + 7 min. standing time. 2 litres: 15–16 min. + 8 min. standing time.

Note Frozen vegetables are cooked at the same time as they are defrosted. For information on all vegetables see the chart on pages 72–7.

REHEATING

One of the biggest boons of a microwave oven is its capacity to reheat food extremely fast without drying it out. Manufacturers estimate that over 80 per cent of ovens are bought mostly for reheating and defrosting. Ensuring foods are heated the right way requires a basic understanding of microwave cooking techniques, but most foods can be reheated in the microwave without loss of quality and flavour. For successful reheating, here are some guidelines for you to follow.

FOR REHEATING SUCCESS

- Microwaves are attracted to fat, sugar and moisture in that order, so foods containing fat or sugar heat more quickly than watery food.
- Undercook rather than overcook – you can always put food back into the oven for extra time.
- Where possible allow foods to stand at room temperature for 10 minutes before microwaving as chilled foods take longer to reheat.
- Reheat main course and meat dishes on MEDIUM-HIGH (70–80%) for the best results. They may become tough if you use HIGH power.
- Cover dishes to retain moisture. Use plastic wrap for moist foods and paper towel for drier ones, for instance crumbed schnitzels.
- Reheat individual meals. For roast meat and vegetable dinners, carve the meat into thin slices. Place on a plain plate (no metal trim) and pour over a gravy or sauce. Choose similar fibred vegetables, such as potatoes and carrots, and then arrange the food in a single layer with the bulkier vegetables and the thicker meat parts to the

outside of the plate. Cover with microwave-safe plastic wrap and heat on MEDIUM-HIGH (70–80%) for 2–3 minutes until the underside of the plate is just warm in the centre.

● Reheat casseroles, covered, on MEDIUM-HIGH (70–80%) and stir several times to distribute the heat evenly during warming time.

● Dishes that cannot be stirred, such as lasagne, should be reheated on MEDIUM (50–60%) rather than HIGH, to avoid toughening the protein ingredients of the dish whilst keeping the pasta moist.

● Reheat vegetables on HIGH (90–100%) for short periods of time. When planning to reheat vegetables, it is wise to undercook them initially so they do not toughen and lose their texture and colour when reheated. Cover and stir vegetables whilst reheating.

● Reheat bread in absorbent non-recycled plain paper towel, to absorb the moisture. Elevate on a roasting rack for better results. Don't over-reheat bread rolls or bread, as they quickly become hard.

● Reheat cooked quiches and pastries on non-recycled plain paper towel. Elevating pastry on a roasting rack helps avoid a soggy result. Pastry items are best reheated on MEDIUM-HIGH (70–80%) and should always be allowed to stand to equalise the heat produced within.

● Moisten pasta or rice dishes with water, wine or sauce before reheating as they dry out easily, especially if refrigerated.

● Stir sauces and custards and reheat on MEDIUM-HIGH (70–80%) to prevent overheating and lumps forming.

● Desserts such as self-saucing puddings and fruit-based crumbles reheat successfully in individual serving bowls. Cover with plastic wrap and heat on MEDIUM-HIGH (70–80%) for 1–2 minutes.

REHEATING GUIDE

Begin by selecting the minimum reheating time. This will prevent overheating and more time can always be added at the end if the reheating is not complete.

FOOD	TECHNIQUE	POWER	TIME
BREAD Roll	From room temp. Wrap single rolls in paper towel. Place on roasting rack. Do not stand or rolls may harden.	HIGH (90–100%)	1 roll: 10–15 sec. 2 rolls: 15–20 sec. 4 rolls: 20–35 sec.

FOOD	TECHNIQUE	POWER	TIME
COOKED FOOD On plate	From room temp. Meat should be well covered with gravy or sauce. Meat and firm vegetables to outer rim of plate. Cover tightly with plastic wrap.	1–2 serves: MEDIUM (50–60%) 4 serves: MEDIUM-HIGH (70–80%)	1 serve: 2–4 min. + standing time. 2 serves: 3–5 min. + standing time. 4 serves: 6–8 min. + standing time.
In serving dish and can be stirred	From fridge. Cover and stir once a minute.	MEDIUM-HIGH (70–80%)	1 serve: 2–4 min. + standing time. 2 serves: 4–6 min. + standing time.
In serving dish and cannot be stirred	From fridge. Cover with plastic wrap. Rotate dish at 2-min. intervals for even reheating.	MEDIUM (50–60%)	1 serve: 5–8 min. + standing time. 2 serves: 9–12 min. + standing time.
MEAT, COOKED In serving dish	From fridge. Place in a single layer and cover with plastic wrap.	MEDIUM (50–60%)	1 serve: 1½–3 min. + standing time. 2 serves: 2½–5 min. + standing time.
Sliced and in serving dish	Cover with gravy or sauce. Cover dish with plastic wrap. Check after every 30 sec. per serving.	MEDIUM (50–60%)	From fridge: 1 serve: 1–3 min. + standing time. From room temp.: 1 serve: 1–2 min. + standing time.

Note Standing time is approximately one-quarter of cooking time.

FOOD	TECHNIQUE	POWER	TIME
Schnitzel	Reheat between paper towel.	MEDIUM-HIGH (70–80%)	1 schnitzel: 2 min. + standing time. 2 schnitzels: 3–3½ min. + standing time.
PASTA	From fridge. Reheat in serving dish. Moisten with a little stock, sauce, cream or butter. Cover with plastic wrap. Do not stir.	MEDIUM-HIGH (70–80%)	1 serve: 2–3 min. + standing time. 2 serves: 4–5 min. + standing time.
Lasagne	As Pasta.	MEDIUM (50–60%)	1 serve: 3–4 min. + standing time. 4 serves: 10–12 min. + standing time.
Pasta with sauce	As Pasta.	MEDIUM-HIGH (70–80%)	1 serve: 3–5 min. + standing time.
PIZZA Whole	From fridge. Elevate on a roasting rack.	MEDIUM (50–60%)	4–5 min. + standing time.
1 slice	As Pizza, whole.	HIGH (90–100%)	1½–2 min. + standing time.
RICE Cooked	As Pasta.	MEDIUM-HIGH (70–80%)	1 serve: 2–3 min. + standing time. 4 serves: 8–10 min. + standing time.
Rice and curry	As Pasta.	MEDIUM-HIGH (70–80%)	1 serve: 3–5 min. + standing time.
VEGE-TABLES	From fridge. Always undercook vegetables initially. Cover with plastic wrap. Stir half-way through reheating.	HIGH (90–100%)	1 serve (½ cup): 1 min. + standing time. 2 serves (1 cup): 1½–2½ min. + standing time.

Note Standing time is approximately one-quarter of cooking time.

GUIDELINES

....

MICROWAVE POWER SETTINGS

Power	Microwave Setting	Conventional Heat
10–20%	WARM	Cool
30–35%	DEFROST	Slow
30–40%	LOW	Moderately Slow
50–60%	MEDIUM	Moderate
70–80%	MEDIUM-HIGH	Moderately Hot
90–100%	HIGH	Hot

READY MEASUREMENTS

STANDARD METRIC MEASURE
1 cup	250 ml
1 tablespoon	20 ml
1 teaspoon	5 ml

(All spoon measurements are level.)

SIMPLE CUP MEASURES (1 cup = 250 ml)

	grams	ounces
breadcrumbs		
dry	125	4½
soft	60	2
butter	250	8¾

	grams	ounces
cheese, grated cheddar	125	4½
flour		
cornflour	130	4¾
plain or self-raising	125	4½
wholemeal	135	4¾
fruit, mixed dried	160	5¾
honey	360	12¾
nuts	125	4½
rice		
brown uncooked	180	6¼
white uncooked	200	7
sugar		
castor	225	7¼
granulated	250	8¾
icing	175	6¾
moist brown	170	6

Food should always be at room temperature before being put in the microwave. If food is taken straight from the fridge it will take longer to cook than the recipe directs.

FISH

The microwave oven cooks fish better than any other way. However, fish cooks almost as fast as it heats so one has to be careful when cooking it. Just a little overcooking can result in dryness.

- Weigh fish and then work out cooking time.
- Cook thin to medium-thick fillets on HIGH (90–100%). Cook thick fillets, cutlets or whole fish on MEDIUM–HIGH (70–80%).
- Make sure fish is properly arranged in the cooking container, with tail ends tucked under to make a uniform thickness. The thickest portions must be placed to the outer edge of the container.
- Select the right cover: plastic wrap or lid for steam or poaching, paper towel or baking paper for baking.
- Test for 'doneness' shortly before the end of cooking time as fish cooks on during standing time. When flesh whitens and flakes easily stop cooking.
- Serve thin fillets immediately. Don't serve whole fish and thicker cuts straight away, but allow to stand, tightly covered, to finish cooking through evenly.
- Eliminate fishy odours from the oven by boiling some lemon slices in a cup of water in the microwave for a few minutes.

Never forget to let food stand after microwaving. Cooking is completed during this time.

FISH COOKING GUIDE

Cook for minimum time at first. Extra cooking can easily be added on at the end if necessary.

FISH	TECHNIQUE	POWER	TIME
Cutlets and steaks (2.5 cm thick)	Elevate dish on roasting rack. Sprinkle with white wine or lemon juice. Season with freshly ground black pepper and herbs. Cover tightly with baking paper.	MEDIUM–HIGH (70–80%)	per 500g: 7 min. + standing time.
Fillets	Place boneless fillets in casserole dish. Sprinkle with lemon juice, dot with butter. Partially cover dish.	MEDIUM–HIGH (70–80%)	per 500 g: 4–5 min. + standing time.
Whole fish, small	Clean and gut. Slash skin several times. Pierce eyes. Place in casserole dish. Season with freshly ground black pepper and melted butter. Partially cover dish.	MEDIUM–HIGH (70–80%)	per 500 g: 4–5 min. + standing time.
Whole fish, large	Slash skin in thick section. Pierce eyes. Season cavity and skin with pepper. Brush with melted butter. Elevate on roasting rack. Loosely cover with baking paper.	MEDIUM–HIGH (70–80%)	per 500 g: 7–10 min. + standing time.

Note Standing time is approximately one-quarter of cooking time.

SALMON PATTIES

An easy recipe for this ever-popular standby.
You can substitute canned tuna for salmon.

500 g mashed potato
1 × 210 g can salmon, drained and bones
  removed
4 spring onions, chopped
2 tablespoons lemon juice
pepper to taste
½ cup crushed corn flakes

METHOD
❶ Mix potato, salmon, spring onions and
   lemon juice together thoroughly. Season
   with pepper.
❷ Shape into 8 patties, 4–5 cm round.
❸ Roll in corn flake crumbs, pressing
   crumbs on firmly.
❹ Place 4 patties on a sheet of absorbent
   paper towel or a roasting rack in a
   circular configuration.
❺ Cook on HIGH (90–100%) for 2 minutes.
   Stand for 30 seconds. Repeat procedure
   for the remaining patties.
❻ Serve with lemon wedges.

VARIATIONS
● Add a small can of drained corn kernels,
  crushed pineapple or asparagus bits to
  potato.
● Add chopped herbs or a dash of Tabasco
  to mixture.

SERVING SUGGESTIONS
● Serve with a salad or mixed green
  vegetables.
● Add 1 teaspoon dill to White Sauce (see
  page 108) and serve over patties.

SERVES 4–6

PREPARATION TIME
25 minutes

COOKING TIME
5 minutes

UTENSIL
Roasting rack

ACCESSORY
Paper towel

EASY TIPS
*Lemon will produce more
juice if first heated on
HIGH (90–100%) for 30–40
seconds. Stand before
squeezing.*

*For mashed potatoes, take
4 medium potatoes. Scrub
and pierce. Place around
edge of turntable and cook
on HIGH (90–100%) for 8–10
minutes, turning over
halfway through cooking.
Stand 2–3 minutes. Potato
skins will then slip off
easily and potato is ready
to mash.*

BAKED LARGE TREVALLY STUFFED WITH TOMATO AND ZUCCHINI

SERVES 4

PREPARATION TIME
10 minutes

COOKING TIME
19 minutes

UTENSIL
Roasting rack

ACCESSORY
Baking paper

EASY TIPS
Tenting baking paper or paper towel over fish when cooking will prevent spatters and keep fish moist without steaming.

Slash the skin of fish to prevent curling.

Shield the tail with foil to prevent overcooking, making sure no foil is touching the oven walls.

Once you learn to cook fish in the microwave you may never do it any other way as the texture of the cooked fish is perfect. A stuffing of vegetables enhances the flavour and appearance of baked fish.

1 whole trevally (about 1 kg), cleaned
1 small onion, finely chopped
1 tomato, diced
1 small zucchini, diced
pinch each of parsley and oregano
freshly ground black pepper

METHOD
1. Slash skin of fish and pierce eyes. Place fish on a roasting rack.
2. Mix vegetables and herbs together.
3. Season cavity with pepper to taste, stuff with vegetables.
4. Wrap fish in baking paper making a tent-shape. Cook on MEDIUM–HIGH (70–80%) for 15 minutes.
5. Stand covered for 4 minutes to complete the cooking process.

VARIATIONS
- Other vegetables may be used, e.g. mushrooms, capsicum.
- Use any fresh herb, e.g. lemon grass, dill.

SERVING SUGGESTION
- Serve with a fresh salad, a bowl of chips and crusty bread.

FLAKE KEBABS

Kebabs are easy to handle as the fish is cut into bite-sized pieces. If the fish is boneless they can be safely served to children or older people.

400 g flake
100 g mushrooms
1 small red capsicum
juice of 1 lemon
freshly ground black pepper

SERVES 4

PREPARATION TIME
10 minutes

COOKING TIME
8–9 minutes

UTENSIL
Roasting rack

ACCESSORY
Bamboo skewers

METHOD
❶ Cut fish, mushrooms and capsicum into approximately 2 cm cubes.
❷ Thread onto 8 bamboo skewers, alternating the fish and vegetables.
❸ Arrange in a spoke-wheel configuration on a roasting rack.
❹ Season with lemon juice and black pepper.
❺ Cook on MEDIUM–HIGH (70–80%) for 4 minutes.
❻ Turn over each kebab from middle to outside and cook another 2–3 minutes. Stand for 1½ minutes.
❼ Sprinkle with extra lemon juice to serve.

VARIATION
● Use snow peas, tomato or button squash with the boneless white fish of your choice.

SERVING SUGGESTION
● Serve with Risotto (see page 68) and accompany with tartare sauce or mayonnaise.

EASY TIP
If you use salt on your fish, add it after cooking, as salt sprinkled over food causes uneven cooking in the microwave.

FRESH FISH IN A FLASH

SERVES 4

PREPARATION TIME
5 minutes

COOKING TIME
7 minutes

UTENSIL
Medium container (1 litre)

Thin fish fillets can be spread with mayonnaise, sour cream or yoghurt to self sauce under a cover whilst cooking in the microwave. Cook for 5 minutes per 500 g on MEDIUM–HIGH (70–80%) for delicious results.

500 g whiting fillets
¼ cup mayonnaise
pinch of chopped fresh herbs (parsley, dill or
  lemon thyme)

METHOD
1. Place fillets in medium microwave container, sprinkle with fresh herbs then spread with mayonnaise.
2. Cover and cook on MEDIUM–HIGH (70–80%) for 5 minutes.
3. Stand for 2 minutes, covered.

VARIATIONS
● Less expensive thin fillets such as trout, John Dory or flathead may be used.
● Vary herbs to suit the fish.
● Add 1 tablespoon capers to mayonnaise.

EASY TIPS
To prevent overcooking, weigh fish carefully before assessing the cooking time. Thick fillets and whole fish take slightly more time than thin fillets. Fish should be opaque at the end of microwave cooking time.

Overlap thin tail ends or fold under for an even thickness to prevent overcooking.

SERVING SUGGESTION
● Serve with rice or pasta and mixed vegetables.

BAKED FRESH TROUT

The kitchen doesn't smell fishy when you microwave-bake fish, and the clean-up is easy as no scouring pads are needed.

2 small trout (about 250–300 g each), cleaned
juice of 1 lemon
freshly ground black pepper
1 tablespoon fresh thyme, finely chopped, to
  garnish

METHOD
❶ Slash skin and pierce eyes of fish. Place on a roasting rack.
❷ Season to taste with pepper and sprinkle with lemon juice.
❸ Cook on MEDIUM–HIGH (70–80%) for 5 minutes, covered loosely with paper towel.
❹ Stand trout covered with foil for 2 minutes to complete the cooking process.
❺ Garnish with herbs and serve.

VARIATIONS
● Sprinkle with white wine.
● Season with fresh herbs and melted butter.
● Garnish with lightly toasted slivered almonds.

SERVING SUGGESTION
● Serve with stir-fry vegetables or fresh salad.

SERVES 4

PREPARATION TIME
5 minutes

COOKING TIME
7 minutes

UTENSIL
Roasting rack

ACCESSORY
Paper towel

EASY TIPS
Arrange small fish in opposite positions for best cooking results, i.e. head to tail, tail to head.

A perfectly cooked fish will break easily when touched with a fork but still retain moisture.

TUNA AND VEGETABLE MORNAY

SERVES 4

PREPARATION TIME
20 minutes

COOKING TIME
12 minutes

UTENSIL
Large container (1.5 litre)

ACCESSORY
Plastic wrap

As well as being the ultimate convenience food, tuna is nutritionally one of the best of all protein foods. Tuna is ideally suited to microwave cooking, maintaining its distinctive flavour and chunky texture.

1 cup White Sauce (see page 108)
1 cup grated cheese
2 × 180 g cans tuna, drained
2 cups blanched vegetables (for example, a
  mixture of beans, carrots and corn)
½ teaspoon Worcestershire sauce

METHOD
❶ Make sauce (see page 108).
❷ Add half the cheese while sauce is hot. Stir in to melt.
❸ Add tuna, vegetables and Worcestershire sauce. Mix well.
❹ Cover and heat on HIGH (90–100%) for 4–5 minutes, stirring twice.
❺ Sprinkle with remaining cheese. Stand for 1 minute and serve.

VARIATION
● Vary the vegetables by using peas, celery, onion, red capsicum, zucchini.

SERVING SUGGESTIONS
● Serve with Steamed Rice (see page 67) or crusty bread.
● Serve with pasta.
● Serve in vol-au-vent shells for special occasions.

EASY TIP
To blanch vegetables in the microwave oven, cut into bite-sized pieces. Place in a shallow dish. Cover tightly with plastic wrap. Cook on HIGH (90–100%) *for 2 minutes. Add to casseroles, stir frys, soups and mornays.*

GARLIC PRAWNS

Fresh is best for this dish, but whether fresh or frozen the flavour of prawns cooked in the microwave is unexcelled. Cooking is speedy and simple, eliminating messy pans to wash, as well as fishy odours in the kitchen.

30 g butter
3–4 cloves garlic, crushed
250 g green prawns, shelled
chopped chives or parsley to garnish
juice of 1 lemon

METHOD

❶ Place butter and garlic in container. Cook on HIGH (90–100%), uncovered, for 1 minute.

❷ Arrange prawns in the base of container in a fan shape with tails towards the centre. Cover loosely with paper towel.

❸ Cook on MEDIUM–HIGH (70–80%) for 2½ minutes, turning prawns over half-way through cooking time.

❹ Pour over lemon juice. Stand 30 seconds and sprinkle with chopped parsley to serve.

VARIATION

● Add finely chopped fresh chilli to butter and garlic for a hot and spicy flavour.

SERVING SUGGESTION

● Serve as an entrée with crusty french bread or fresh buttered brown bread.

SERVES 4

PREPARATION TIME
20 minutes

COOKING TIME
4 minutes

UTENSIL
Medium container (1 litre)

ACCESSORY
Paper towel

EASY TIPS
Before cooking, prepare prawns by making a slit down the back of each prawn and removing the dark vein.

Cloves of garlic can be peeled easily by placing the cloves on the turntable and heating for 10 seconds per clove on HIGH (90–100%). The garlic will then slip out of its skin.

SWISS FISH

SERVES 4

PREPARATION TIME
5 minutes

COOKING TIME
10 minutes

UTENSILS
Roasting rack
Small bowl

ACCESSORIES
Plastic wrap
Aluminium foil

Fish cooked in the microwave stays moist and cooks through evenly provided it is not overcooked. For thick cutlets or fillets, cook on MEDIUM–HIGH (70–80%), test, then briefly stand before serving with a sauce.

500 g cutlets (salmon, blue eye or trevally)
⅓ cup cream
100 g swiss cheese, grated
2 teaspoons whole grain mustard

METHOD

❶ Place cutlets on a roasting rack; cover with plastic wrap and cook on MEDIUM–HIGH (70–80%) for 7 minutes, turning over once.

❷ Stand, covered with foil, while preparing sauce.

❸ Bring cream to the boil in a small bowl on MEDIUM–HIGH (70–80%) for approximately 1½ minutes.

❹ Add cheese and stir to melt. Add any juices from the fish.

❺ Cook for 1 minute on MEDIUM (50–60%) until cheese is completely melted. Stir in mustard and pour over fish to serve.

VARIATION

● Add dry white wine or dry sherry to cream.

SERVING SUGGESTIONS

● Serve with salad or mixed vegetables.
● Serve on a bed of plain rice.

EASY TIPS
All fish continues to cook on briefly after microwaving. Allow for this when testing for 'doneness'.

Fish cutlets are sufficiently cooked once the flesh begins to whiten and flake at the thickest part when tested with a fork.

CHICKEN

Poultry makes up over 16 per cent of all main dishes served in Australian homes. Microwave-cooked poultry is moist and tender. The microwave oven can successfully roast, casserole or cook poultry with sauce. If you wish to cook it fat-free, remove most of the skin and fat before cooking.

A microwave thermometer is a useful accessory when cooking poultry, as the internal temperature can then be checked to ensure the cooking has been sufficient to kill all bacteria.

- Defrost frozen birds fully, clean well and thoroughly dry with paper towel before cooking.
- Do not stuff birds with raw stuffing. The short microwave cooking times may not be enough to cook stuffing thoroughly, so you cook the stuffing *before* you put it in the bird.
- Weigh carefully, after stuffing, and then calculate timing so chicken will reach 70°C and therefore be perfectly cooked.
- Cover portions of poultry, i.e. legs and wings, with small pieces of smooth foil to shield and prevent overcooking. Make sure foil does not touch the oven walls and cause arcing.
- Brush poultry all over with a glaze or sauce to enhance its colour.
- Use your oven variables for best results, for instance, reduce the power to MEDIUM (50–60%) for cooking large birds.
- Drain excess fats and juices during cooking as they accumulate. This will help to shorten cooking time and keep the oven clean.
- Small boneless chicken pieces cook more evenly, and faster, than larger pieces.
- Stir chicken casseroles once or twice during cooking time to equalise

the temperature, remembering that small pieces of chicken in liquid will cook more quickly than a whole chicken.

● Don't forget the correct arrangement of poultry pieces – that is, placed in a single layer with the thicker sections towards the outside of the container.

● Always stand poultry before serving.

CHICKEN COOKING GUIDE

Cook for the minimum time at first. Extra cooking can easily be added on at the end if necessary.

FOOD	TECHNIQUE	POWER	TIME
Chicken, whole	Cook any stuffing before filling bird. Brush bird with soy or teriyaki sauce. Elevate on roasting rack loosely covered with paper towel. Internal temp. should be 70°C at end of cooking time and 73°C at end of standing time.	HIGH (90–100%)	per 500 g: 10 min. + standing time. Add 2 min. cooking time per bird if stuffed.
Chicken fillets	Brush with equal parts chicken stock and dry sherry. Elevate on roasting rack loosely covered with paper towel. Internal temp. should be 70°C at end of cooking time and 73°C at end of standing time.	HIGH (90–100%) followed by MEDIUM–HIGH (70–80%)	per 500 g: 5 min. on HIGH, then 6–7 min. on MEDIUM–HIGH + standing time.
Chicken maryland	Place thicker portions to outer edge of roasting rack. Brush with equal parts of chicken stock and soy sauce sweetened with 1 teaspoon honey. Cover loosely with paper towel. Internal temp. should be 70°C at end of cooking time and 73°C at end of standing time.	HIGH (90–100%)	per 500 g: 7 min. + standing time.
Chicken wings/ ribs	As Chicken maryland	MEDIUM– HIGH (70–80%)	per 500 g: 5–6 min. + standing time.

Note Standing time is approximately one-quarter of cooking time.

APRICOT CHICKEN

This is a popular and economical meal that can be cooked ahead. Cooked poultry can be kept refrigerated for three or four days. As soon as cool, seal well in an airtight container and chill.

1 × 425 g can apricot halves
1 × 40 g packet dried french onion soup
500 g skinless chicken chops
1 tablespoon chopped, fresh parsley

METHOD
❶ Drain apricot juice into a large container and stir in soup.
❷ Add chicken chops and apricot pieces. Cover the container.
❸ Cook on HIGH (90–100%) for 10 minutes, stirring once.
❹ Stand for 4 minutes.
❺ Garnish with parsley and serve.

VARIATION
● Use canned sliced mangoes.

SERVING SUGGESTION
● Serve with rice and vegetables or salad.

SERVES 4

PREPARATION TIME
2 minutes

COOKING TIME
14 minutes

UTENSIL
Large container (1.5 litre)

EASY TIPS
Poultry cooks more evenly if covered during microwave cooking.

Small pieces of chicken in liquid stock cook more quickly than a whole chicken, or large pieces.

Rearrange chicken pieces during cooking. Turn poultry over and move less cooked portions towards the outside of the container.

CHICKEN STIR FRY

SERVES 4

PREPARATION TIME
5 minutes

COOKING TIME
10 minutes

UTENSIL
Large container (1.5 litre)

ACCESSORIES
Paper towel
Plastic wrap

An inexpensive, easy-to-make family favourite that can be prepared quickly. It's versatile too, as you can vary the vegetables.

500 g chicken wings, cut into two at the joint
4 spring onions, sliced diagonally
1 carrot, sliced
¼ cup chicken stock
2 tablespoons oyster sauce
2 teaspoons cornflour

METHOD

❶ Cook wings in the large container on HIGH (90–100%) for 5 minutes, covered with paper towel. Set chicken aside.

❷ Cook vegetables in the container lid on HIGH (90–100%) for 2 minutes, covered with plastic wrap.

❸ Add vegetables to chicken.

❹ Mix stock with oyster sauce and cornflour. Pour over chicken. Cover.

❺ Cook on HIGH (90–100%) for 2–3 minutes, stirring occasionally to thicken sauce and re-heat evenly.

VARIATION

● Use snow peas and sliced red capsicum as vegetables, or for a lively colour use red, green and yellow capsicums when in season.

EASY TIP
Place stir-fried left-overs on a plate, cover loosely with plastic wrap and cook on MEDIUM–HIGH (70–80%) for 1½–2 minutes, until heated through. Stir-fried vegetables should still be crisp.

SERVING SUGGESTION

● Serve with Steamed Rice (see page 67) or instant noodles.

OLD-FASHIONED CHICKEN SOUP

This heart-warming home-made soup can be made in just half an hour. You can cook, serve, refrigerate and reheat all in the same container. Use the cooked chicken for sandwiches or freeze for standby meals.

1.25 kg chicken, cleaned
1 large onion, chopped
1 carrot, sliced
1 stick celery, sliced
1 litre hot water
1 tablespoon finely chopped parsley
salt and pepper to taste

METHOD
❶ Place all ingredients together in a large container and cover.
❷ Cook on HIGH (90–100%) for 30 minutes in the centre of the turntable.
❸ Remove the chicken. Take off breast and thigh and set aside. Break off flesh from wings, legs and carcass and return this meat to soup.
❹ Season to taste and garnish with parsley to serve.

VARIATIONS
● Use the cooked meat for Mustard Sauced Chicken (see page 44).
● Drain stock from chicken and vegetables. Freeze and use when chicken stock is required for casseroles, sauces or risotto.
● Add instant noodles to the soup and reheat.

SERVING SUGGESTION
● Serve with crusty bread or garlic bread.

SERVES 4

PREPARATION TIME
5 minutes

COOKING TIME
30 minutes

UTENSIL
*Extra-large container
(2.25 litre)*

EASY TIP
Adding hot water or stock instead of cold shortens the cooking time of soups made in the microwave oven.

ORIENTAL-STYLE CHICKEN BALLS

SERVES 4

PREPARATION TIME
5 minutes

COOKING TIME
9 minutes

UTENSIL
Roasting rack

These chicken balls are nutritious and quick to cook and have the added appeal of being low in kilojoules.

1 kg minced chicken
1 egg
20 g fresh ginger, grated
1 tablespoon sesame seeds, toasted
1 cup rolled oats
3 spring onions, chopped
extra seeds, toasted

METHOD
❶ Mix all ingredients together except extra sesame seeds. Roll into 12 balls. Sprinkle with extra seeds.
❷ Place around the edge of a roasting rack.
❸ Cook on HIGH (90–100%) for 7 minutes. Rotate balls once during cooking.
❹ Stand for 2 minutes before serving.

VARIATION
● Use 1 teaspoon Worcestershire sauce and ground black pepper in place of ginger.

SERVING SUGGESTION
● Serve with Oriental Sauce (see page 110), Vegetable Medley (see page 78) and Steamed Rice (see page 67).

EASY TIPS
Rotating means foods are turned round rather than over, to ensure even cooking. This is usually a quarter or a half turn.

To toast sesame seeds, put on an ovenable glass plate and cook on HIGH (90–100%) for 2–3 minutes, stirring regularly.

MARYLANDS FOR TWO WITH LEMON SAUCE

Readily obtainable, chicken marylands make a speedy roast meal for two. Place the thicker portions outwards and the thin ends inwards to ensure even cooking results.

2 chicken marylands (about 750 g) rinsed, dried
   and pierced
2 tablespoons chopped fresh herbs (e.g. chives or
   spring onions), for garnish
Baste
¼ cup lemon juice
¼ cup light soy sauce
2 teaspoons honey
Lemon Sauce
reserved pan juice
1 teaspoon cornflour

METHOD

1 Mix all ingredients of baste together. Brush chicken pieces thoroughly with baste, using all the fluid.

2 Elevate on a roasting rack and cover loosely with paper towel.

3 Cook on HIGH (90–100%) for 7 minutes then remove from oven. Take off paper towel and pour juices into a small jug.

4 Stand chicken on a serving dish covered with foil whilst you make the sauce.

5 Blend cornflour with a little of the reserved pan juices in small bowl, then add to jug, stirring well.

6 Cook sauce on MEDIUM–HIGH (70–80%) for 1 minute until thickened.

7 Spoon sauce over chicken and add garnish.

SERVING SUGGESTION

● Serve with Fried Rice (see page 69) and a green salad.

SERVES 2

PREPARATION TIME
5 minutes

COOKING TIME
10 minutes

UTENSIL
Roasting rack

ACCESSORIES
Paper towel
Aluminium foil

EASY TIPS
Larger quantities of chicken will take longer to cook, therefore it is sometimes better to cook 2 batches of smaller quantities of chicken pieces.

Marinating marylands for several hours in the baste improves the colour and flavour of the chicken when cooked.

ROAST CHICKEN

SERVES 4

PREPARATION TIME
10 minutes

COOKING TIME
35 minutes

UTENSILS
Roasting rack
Small container (400 ml)

ACCESSORIES
Paper towel
Aluminium foil

Chicken is wonderfully tasty as well as quick and easy when cooked in the microwave oven. When cooking a stuffed bird you will need to add approximately 2 minutes to the calculated cooking time of an unstuffed bird.

1.25 kg chicken, cleaned, dried and pierced
Stuffing
1 onion, chopped
1 tablespoon butter
2 rashers bacon, chopped
½ cup breadcrumbs
mixed herbs
Baste
2 tablespoons tomato sauce
1 tablespoon soy sauce

METHOD

❶ Cook onion and butter for stuffing for 1 minute on HIGH (90–100%) in a small container.

❷ Add bacon and cook for 2 minutes on HIGH (90–100%).

❸ Stir in breadcrumbs and herbs. Place stuffing in chicken cavity.

❹ Mix tomato and soy sauces together for baste. Brush all over chicken.

❺ Cook chicken breast-side up on HIGH (90–100%) for 22–25 minutes, basting once.

❻ After cooking cover with foil and allow to stand for at least 10 minutes to complete the cooking process. The foil will keep the chicken hot while you prepare the rest of the meal.

EASY TIPS
Chicken can be turned over half-way through cooking if preferred.

Do not stuff poultry ahead of cooking time. For convenience you can pre-cook stuffing ready to stuff the bird just prior to its cooking time.

SERVING SUGGESTION
● Serve with Vegetable Medley (see page 78) and Risotto (see page 68).

MUSTARD SAUCED CHICKEN

Cooked chicken pieces, particularly the meaty breasts, are delicious when teamed with flavoursome sauce. Despite the speed of microwave cooking, chicken flesh always remains tender and succulent when heated through on MEDIUM–HIGH (70–80%).

½ cup cream
2 teaspoons grain mustard
4 cooked boneless chicken pieces (about 400 g)
chopped fresh herbs (parsley, chives or coriander)

METHOD

❶ Stir cream and mustard together in a small container. Warm on MEDIUM (50–60%) for 1 minute to blend.

❷ Place chicken on a pie plate (you can use chicken from Old-fashioned Chicken Soup on page 40). Pour sauce over. Cover with plastic wrap.

❸ Heat on MEDIUM–HIGH (50–60%) for 2–3 minutes.

❹ Serve sprinkled with freshly chopped herbs.

VARIATION

● Instead of grain mustard, use mustard sauce or paste.

SERVING SUGGESTION

● Serve with Steamed Rice (see page 67), freshly cooked pasta or vegetables.

SERVES 4

PREPARATION TIME
3–4 minutes

COOKING TIME
3–4 minutes

UTENSILS
Small container (400 ml)
Ovenable glass pie plate

ACCESSORY
Plastic wrap

EASY TIPS
Remove skin from chicken to reduce fat in this recipe.

Skinning chicken before microwaving with a sauce allows more sauce flavour to penetrate the chicken.

To prevent chicken from toughening, season it with salt at the end of cooking.

CHICKEN FILLETS ANYTIME

SERVES 4

PREPARATION TIME
2 minutes

COOKING TIME
8 minutes

UTENSILS
Medium container (1 litre)
Small ovenable glass jug

Skinless chicken fillets are versatile and inexpensive as there is no wastage. Chicken is considered a 'white meat' and skinless chicken breasts contain very little fat after cooking.

500 g skinless chicken fillets
2 tablespoons savoury plum sauce

METHOD
❶ Arrange fillets in medium container, overlapping thin tails. Pierce each in several places.
❷ Cover, cook on MEDIUM–HIGH (70–80%) for 5–6 minutes, turning over once during cooking.
❸ Stand covered for 2 minutes to finish cooking.
❹ Mix plum sauce with juices from chicken in small ovenable glass jug and warm on MEDIUM–HIGH (70–80%) to blend.
❺ Spoon over cooked fillets and serve.

VARIATION
● Allow cooked chicken fillets to cool, cube and mix with chopped celery, walnuts and mayonnaise to make a 'chicken waldorf salad'.

EASY TIPS
Boneless chicken fillets cook more quickly in the microwave than breast on the bone.

Pierce chicken to avoid 'popping'.

If chicken pieces are unevenly shaped you will need to do a little rearranging during microwaving.

SERVING SUGGESTION
● Arrange chicken fillet on a bed of rice and serve with White Sauce (see page 108) and Fresh Green Beans (see page 85).

CHICKEN STROGANOFF

Chicken stroganoff updates a classic Russian dish, traditionally made with thinly sliced beef, coated with a cream sauce.

500 g skinned chicken fillets
1 onion, sliced
1 tablespoon tomato paste
½ cup sour cream
1 × 425 g can champignons, drained
chopped chives or parsley, to garnish

METHOD

❶ Cut chicken into thin strips. Place around the edge of large container, cover. Cook on HIGH (90–100%) for 4 minutes, stirring once.

❷ Stand chicken for 1 minute, covered.

❸ Blanch onion slices, closely covered with plastic wrap, by cooking on HIGH (90–100%) for 1 minute.

❹ Stir tomato paste into juices from chicken. Add sour cream, onions and champignons, then toss all the ingredients together. Cover and cook on MEDIUM–HIGH (70–80%) for 3–4 minutes, stirring twice. Stand 1 minute. Sprinkle with chopped chives or parsley and serve.

VARIATION

● Add a can of well-drained asparagus cuts.

SERVING SUGGESTION

● Serve with Steamed Rice (see page 68).

SERVES 4

PREPARATION TIME
6 minutes

COOKING TIME
10 minutes

UTENSIL
Large container (1.5 litre)

ACCESSORY
Plastic wrap

EASY TIPS
Toss chicken in sweet paprika before cooking to give colour and flavour.

Arranging chicken strips in a doughnut shape reduces cooking time and ensures even cooking.

MEAT

Common sense dictates the best way to cook meat in the microwave oven. Ask yourself how you cooked your favourite cut conventionally, and then see if you can employ the same technique. Remember, the microwave can perform most of the functions of conventional cooking except deep frying, which is not recommended as the heat of the oil cannot be controlled. You can roast, stir fry, casserole or simmer in the microwave.

- Select the appropriate technique to suit your needs, using the charts (pages 48–52) to calculate the correct timing.
- Remove excess fat as it will attract the microwaves, but retain some to provide flavour, juice and assist in browning.
- Meat will brown better if marinated before cooking. Add glazes for colour and flavour, as well as the herbs of your choice, but use herbs sparingly as they retain a stronger flavour after microwaving than if cooked conventionally.
- Try to use tender cuts of meat for microwave cooking as they cook better than less tender cuts that may need moisture and long, slow cooking to soften their connective tissue.
- Cheaper meat cuts benefit from marinating overnight before cooking.
- Cut casserole meat into uniform-sized pieces for even cooking.
- Tent meat with paper towel or baking paper (i.e. wrap loosely in a tent shape) to prevent the oven steaming and being spattered.
- Do not salt meat before microwaving as the salt draws out moisture and toughens meat. If a dish needs salt, add it at the table.
- Do roast meat in the microwave oven – you will have juicy results

and there is little shrinkage – but elevate it on a roasting rack to keep the meat above the fat and juices and improve its appearance.

● You may have to change the power level during meat cooking for juicy results. For instance, you may start meat cooking on HIGH (90–100%) for 5–10 minutes, then reduce to MEDIUM (50–60%) power.

● Turn meat once or twice during cooking time, depending on the size and thickness of the cut.

● Stir casseroles through during cooking to distribute the heat.

● Remember long, slow simmering (30–40%) is recommended for cuts like silverside, which should only be lightly salted. Although little time is saved by simmering in the microwave oven rather than conventionally it does save money, as the running cost is approximately one-third the running cost of a large conventional hot plate.

● Meats cooked longer than 10 minutes will brown like those cooked conventionally, but will not crispen. You can achieve crisping using a combination of microwave and conventional methods.

● Remember the importance of standing time when cooking meat. Because most meats are dense, the temperature will equalise during this time and the food completes its cooking.

MEAT COOKING GUIDE

Cook for the minimum time to start with. It is easy to add on a few minutes extra cooking at the end if needed.

FOOD	TECHNIQUE	POWER	TIME
BACON Middle	Remove rind. Elevate on roasting rack and cover with paper towel.	HIGH (90–100%)	2 rashers: 2½–3 min. + 2 min. standing time. 4 rashers: 4½–5 min. + 2 min. standing time. 6 rashers: 6–7 min. + 2 min. standing time.

Note Standing time is approximately one-quarter of cooking time.

FOOD	TECHNIQUE	POWER	TIME
Streaky	Remove rind. Elevate on roasting rack and cover with paper towel.	HIGH (90–100%)	2 rashers: 1½–2 min. + 2 min. standing time. 4 rashers: 3–4 min. + 2 min. standing time. 6 rashers: 5–6 min. + 2 min. standing time.
BEEF Mince	Cook on roasting rack.	MEDIUM– HIGH (70–80%)	per 500 g: 10 min. + standing time.
Open roasting – slender cuts (fillet, scotch fillet, T-bone)	Place trimmed meat, fat side down, on roasting rack. Cover with paper towel. Turn meat over half-way through cooking. For rare beef, internal temp. should be 50°C at end of cooking, 55°C after standing. For medium beef, internal temp. should be 55°C at end of cooking, 65°C after standing. For well done beef, internal temp. should be 65°C at end of cooking, 75°C after standing.	MEDIUM– HIGH (70–80%)	For rare beef, per 500 g: 6 min. + standing time. For medium beef, per 500 g: 7–8 min. + standing time. For well done beef, per 500 g: 9–10 min. + standing time.
Open roasting – thick roasts (rump, scotch fillet, large sirloin, topside)	Place trimmed meat, fat side down, on roasting rack. Cover with paper towel. Turn meat over half-way through cooking. For rare beef, internal temp. should be 50°C at end of cooking, 55–60°C after standing. For medium beef, internal temp. should be 55°C at end of cooking, 60–65°C after standing. For well done beef, internal temp. should be 65°C at end of cooking, 70–75°C after standing.	HIGH (90–100%) for first 5 min. up to 2 kg; for first 10 min. over 2 kg, then MEDIUM– HIGH (70–80%).	For rare beef, per 500 g: 8 min. + standing time. For medium beef, per 500 g: 9–10 min. + standing time. For well-done beef, per 500 g: 10–12 min. + standing time.

Note Standing time is approximately one-quarter of cooking time.

FOOD	TECHNIQUE	POWER	TIME
Oven bag roasting (blade, rolled beef, round steak, fresh silverside, skirt steak)	Dry meat with absorbent paper. Coat lightly with butter and a flour. Place meat in bag, tie loosely with a rubber band (not metal tie) and place on roasting rack. Pierce bag near tie to allow steam to escape. Turn over half-way through cooking. Remove from bag and cover with foil to stand. For medium beef, internal temp. should be 55°C at end of cooking, 60–65°C after standing. For well done beef, internal temp. should be 65°C at end of cooking, 70–75°C after standing.	LOW (30–40%)	For medium beef, per 500 g: 15–16 min. + 15 min. standing time. For well done beef, per 500 g: 19–20 min. + 15 min. standing time.
LAMB Boneless roast (tender spring lamb)	Do not roast a piece of lamb larger than 2.5 kg. Glaze lamb if desired, elevate on roasting rack, cover with paper towel. Turn half-way through cooking. Lamb roasts should stand, covered, for 10–15 min. Internal temp. should be 60°C at end of cooking time.	HIGH (90–100%) followed by MEDIUM–HIGH (70–80%)	per 500 g: 10 min. on HIGH, then 8–9 min. on MEDIUM–HIGH + standing time.
Chump chops	Trim and put in casserole dish, layering with parboiled, thinly sliced potatoes and onions. Cover.	MEDIUM (50–60%)	per 500 g: 10 min. + standing time.
Cubed	Cubes for curries and casseroles should be 1½–2cm. Cook covered. Meat requires stirring during cooking.	MEDIUM (50–60%)	per 500 g: 10 min. + standing time.
Fillet	Glaze. Cook elevated on a roasting rack, loosely covered with paper towel. Internal temp. should be 60°C at end of cooking time.	MEDIUM–HIGH (70–80%)	per 500 g: 6–7 min. + standing time.

Note Standing time is approximately one-quarter of cooking time.

FOOD	TECHNIQUE	POWER	TIME
Leg roast	Coat leg with mixture of breadcrumbs, chopped parsley and thyme and sprinkle with paprika. Elevate on roasting rack with thicker portion of meat to outer edge. Internal temp. should be 60°C at end of cooking time.	HIGH (90–100%) followed by MEDIUM-HIGH (70–80%)	per 500 g: 10 min. on HIGH, followed by 9–10 min. on MEDIUM-HIGH + standing time.
Leg steak	Pound to an even thickness and brush with melted butter and paprika. Place in circle on a roasting rack.	MEDIUM-HIGH (70–80%)	per 500 g: 5–6 min. + standing time.
Midloin chops	Place bone ends towards centre of oven.	HIGH (90–100%)	per 500 g: 7–8 min. + standing time.
PORK Boneless loin roast	If stuffing roast use precooked stuffing. Trim meat of fat. Cook on HIGH, then MEDIUM. Always let pork roasts stand for at least 20 minutes. Internal temp. should be 76°C at end of cooking and 82–85°C after standing time.	HIGH (90–100%) followed by MEDIUM (50–60%)	12–13 min. per 500 g. Begin on HIGH for 10 min. then reduce to MEDIUM for rest of cooking time + standing time.
Cubes		HIGH (90–100%) to seal followed by MEDIUM (50–60%)	per 500 g: 10 min. + standing time.
Leg roast	Thick end towards edge of turntable. Elevate on roasting rack. Baste. Internal temp. should be 76°C at end of cooking and 82–85°C after standing time.	HIGH (90–100%) for first 12 min. then MEDIUM-HIGH (70–80%).	per 500 g: 12–13 min. + standing time.

Note Standing time is approximately one-quarter of cooking time.

FOOD	TECHNIQUE	POWER	TIME
Loin fillet	Marinate for 1–2 hours before cooking. Elevate on a roasting rack and baste often. Internal temp. should be 76°C at end of cooking and 82–85°C after standing time.	MEDIUM–HIGH (70–80%)	per 500 g: 8–10 min. + standing time.
SAUSAGES Thick	Pierce, elevate on roasting rack, cover with paper towel. Turn over half-way through cooking time.	HIGH (90–100%)	2 sausages: 2 min. + 2 min. standing time. 4 sausages: 7–8 min. + 3 min. standing time.
Thin	As Sausages, Thick	HIGH (90–100%)	2 sausages: 2 min. + 2 min. standing time. 4 sausages: 5 min. + 3 min. standing time.
VEAL Cubes (casserole veal and cubed shank)	Pound to tenderise. Prick cubes, marinate for several hours, and stir during cooking.	MEDIUM (50–60%) followed by LOW (30–40%)	5 min. on MEDIUM, then 7 min. per 500 g on LOW + standing time.
Fillet	Marinate in wine for several hours and bake elevated on roasting rack, covered with a paper towel. Internal temp. should be 70°C at end of cooking.	HIGH (90–100%) followed by MEDIUM (50–60%)	5 min. on HIGH, then 3–5 min. per 500 g. on MEDIUM + standing time.
Loin or shoulder roast, boned	Stuff and skewer to secure. Glaze with sauce. Internal temp. should be 70°C at end of cooking.	HIGH (90–100%) followed by MEDIUM (50–60%)	HIGH for first 5 min. then 5–7 min. per 500 g. on MEDIUM + standing time.

Note Standing time is approximately one-quarter of cooking time.

MEATLOAF MADE EASY

SERVES 6–8

PREPARATION TIME
5 minutes

COOKING TIME
21 minutes

UTENSILS
Cake ring pan
Roasting rack
Small bowl

ACCESSORY
Paper towel

EASY TIP
To pre-brown and drain fat from minced beef before cooking, use a microwave colander. Crumble ground beef into the colander, cover loosely with paper towel. Place the colander in a microwave container and for 500 g meat cook on HIGH (90–100%) for 5 minutes.

Minced beef is the basis for many recipes and is a regular food in many homes. It is a regular for microwave cooking too as it's economical, tender and flexible. Other ground meats such as lamb, pork or veal may be substituted for beef.

1 kg minced beef
1 large onion, grated
1 egg, beaten
1 × 50 g packet dried tomato soup
⅓ cup dry breadcumbs
Sauce
⅓ cup tomato sauce
1 tablespoon vinegar
1 tablespoon brown sugar

METHOD
1. Mix all meatloaf ingredients together thoroughly. Season to taste.
2. Press firmly into a ring pan, cover loosely with paper towel.
3. Cook, elevated on roasting rack, on MEDIUM–HIGH (70–80%) for 15 minutes.
4. Stand covered for 5 minutes.
5. To make sauce, mix tomato sauce, vinegar and brown sugar together in a small bowl. Heat on HIGH (90–100%) for 1 minute. Pour over meatloaf.

VARIATIONS
- Any flavour soup may be used.
- Add chopped herbs, grated carrot or corn kernels to meat mixture.
- Top with chutney instead of sauce.
- Mixture can be shaped into balls and cooked in a ring pan for quick meatballs.

CORNED SILVERSIDE

Hot or cold, silverside is always popular and oven bag roasting is ideal for this less tender cut of meat.

1.5 kg corned silverside
1 cup water
¼ cup vinegar
1 onion, peeled and studded with 4 cloves
3 bay leaves

METHOD

❶ Soak meat for 30 minutes. Drain.

❷ Place meat in oven bag with water, vinegar, onion and bay leaf. Secure the bag with a rubber band and pierce a couple of holes near the top. Place bag in microwave container.

❸ Microwave on HIGH (90–100%) for 10 minutes, then reduce power to DEFROST (30–35%) and cook for 20 minutes per 500 g, carefully turning meat over once during cooking. Test for doneness: meat should be soft when pierced with skewer. Cook longer if necessary. Stand for 10 minutes.

VARIATION

● Baste well with the mustard of your choice and cook with vegetables such as onions, carrots and celery to flavour the meat.

SERVING SUGGESTIONS

● Serve with a light white sauce with parsley.
● Serve with white sauce seasoned with mustard.
● Serve cold with chutney or pickles.

SERVES 8

PREPARATION TIME
30 minutes

COOKING TIME
80 minutes

UTENSIL
Extra-large container (2.25 litre)

ACCESSORY
Oven bag

EASY TIP
Secure oven bags loosely with a rubber band or string. Do not use metal tie. Puncture bag twice at the top of the bag to allow steam to release. Meat should be skewer-soft at the end of cooking time.

MINI TOPSIDE OR ROUND LAMB ROAST

SERVES 2–4

COOKING TIME
24 minutes

UTENSIL
Roasting rack

ACCESSORY
Aluminium foil

Great for one or two people. Trim lamb roasts cook beautifully when baked in the microwave oven. Because of the speed these smaller roasts cook, standing time is essential to complete the cooking of the meat.

450 g topside – mini lamb roast
½ cup fruit chutney

METHOD
❶ Place meat on roasting rack and cook on MEDIUM–HIGH (70–80%) for 7 minutes, for medium cooked meat, turning over once.
❷ Wrap in foil and stand for 15 minutes.
❸ Mix any meat juices with chutney and cook on HIGH (90–100%) for 1–2 minutes.
❹ Pour over meat, slice and serve.

VARIATIONS
● Any flavoured chutney may be used.
● Use ⅓ cup wholegrain mustard instead of chutney.
● Baste with mint jelly.

SERVING SUGGESTION
● Serve with a Vegetable Medley (see page 78) or Steamed Rice (see page 67).

EASY TIPS
Cook for an extra 2 minutes for well done meat.

Cover with paper towel to absorb any splatters during cooking.

Use standing time to cook vegetables or rice.

BONED ROAST LAMB

Roasting lamb in the microwave gives juicy results with little shrinkage if you use a suitable cut of meat and the variable powers. It's best to select a boneless cut that can be rolled into a uniform shape for even cooking.

1 kg boned lamb, trimmed of fat
30 g butter
1 small onion, grated
1 cup fresh breadcrumbs
small sprig fresh rosemary

SERVES 4–6

PREPARATION TIME
10 minutes

COOKING TIME
35–40 minutes

UTENSILS
Roasting rack
Small bowl

ACCESSORIES
Aluminium foil
Paper towel

METHOD

❶ Trim as much fat from the lamb as possible.

❷ Place butter and onion in a small bowl, cover and cook on HIGH (90–100%) for 1 minute. Mix in breadcrumbs and chopped rosemary.

❸ Press stuffing into boned cavity of meat.

❹ Re-roll meat encasing stuffing and secure with rubber bands or string.

❺ Place on a roasting rack, cover loosely with paper towel and cook on HIGH (90–100%) for 10 minutes. Drain juices and reserve them.

❻ Turn roast over, cook on MEDIUM–HIGH (70–80%) for 15 minutes (for medium) or 20 minutes (for well done).

❼ Cover with foil and let stand for 10 minutes whilst you make gravy (see page 111).

VARIATIONS

● Add chopped dried apricots or prunes to stuffing mixture.

● Baste with equal parts of dry sherry and soy sauce.

EASY TIP
When roasting in the microwave oven, trim off the fat because it attracts more microwaves than meat. For this reason meat with fat on will cook at a slower rate than a trimmed joint.

LAMB RACKS

SERVES 4

PREPARATION TIME
8 minutes

COOKING TIME
16 minutes

UTENSILS
Roasting rack
Small bowl

ACCESSORY
Aluminium foil

Succulent racks of lamb cook well in the microwave, provided you remember that bone is an excellent conductor of heat and will cause the surrounding meat to overcook if you have not weighed and timed your racks carefully.

4 × 3 cutlet racks of lamb (approximately 750 g in all)
1 clove garlic, sliced
2 tablespoons mint jelly

METHOD
1. Trim lamb very well. Arrange 2 racks to interlock and place on edge of a roasting rack. Repeat with other racks and place on the opposite side of the roasting rack. Stud with sliced garlic.
2. Soften mint jelly in a small bowl on HIGH (90–100%) for 30 seconds. Brush liberally over meat.
3. Cook on MEDIUM–HIGH (70–80%) for 5 minutes.
4. Rotate both sets of racks. Brush well with sauce and cook for another 5–6 minutes on MEDIUM–HIGH (70–80%).
5. Stand covered with foil for 5 minutes before serving.

VARIATIONS
● Add a little mustard to mint jelly.
● Brush meat with a mixture of honey and soy.

SERVING SUGGESTION
● Serve with a Vegetable Medley (see page 78) or a stir fry of vegetables.

EASY TIP
Small roasts are best cooked on MEDIUM–HIGH (70–80%) for the entire cooking time. Allow 5–10 minutes standing time to complete the cooking and utilise this time to cook the vegetables of your choice.

PORK CURRY

Diced pork is an accessible and versatile cut of meat, suitable for curries, quick stir frys and, when well marinated, barbecued on bamboo skewers. Halve the size of the cubes for curry or stir frys and pierce the meat all over for more even cooking results.

1 large onion, diced
1 tablespoon oil
750 g pork, pounded and cut into 3 cm cubes
1 × 285 g can curry sauce of your choice
¼ cup sultanas

METHOD

1 Cook onion in oil for 2 minutes on HIGH (90–100%) in a large microware container.

2 Remove onion and place meat in container. Cover and cook on HIGH (90–100%) for 5 minutes, stirring once.

3 Return onion to container. Stir in curry sauce and sultanas.

4 Cover and cook on MEDIUM (50–60%) for 10–12 minutes, stirring once or twice.

5 Stand for 5 minutes and serve.

VARIATIONS

● Stir in ¼ cup coconut cream on serving.
● Use diced lamb or chicken instead of pork.

SERVING SUGGESTION

● Serve with Steamed Rice (see page 67) and pappadams.

SERVES 4

PREPARATION TIME
3 minutes

COOKING TIME
22 minutes

UTENSIL
Large container (1.5 litre)

EASY TIPS
For 'melt in the mouth' pork, beat the surface of the cubes to break up some of the connective tissue.

For best casserole results cook on MEDIUM (50–60%) or LOW (30–40%) power until soft.

PORK FILLETS

SERVES 4

PREPARATION TIME
1 hour

COOKING TIME
16 minutes

UTENSIL
Roasting rack
Ovenable glass jug

ACCESSORY
Aluminium foil

New-fashioned pork is lean and pork fillets make ideal small roasts to cook in the microwave oven. Marinating before cooking enhances the colour and flavour of these nutritious, tender fillets.

¼ cup red wine
2 tablespoons savoury plum sauce
2 spring onions, chopped
2 pork fillets (about 500 g)
1 tablespoon cornflour

METHOD

❶ Mix red wine, plum sauce and spring onions together. Marinate pork in liquid for 1 hour. Remove fillets and reserve marinade.

❷ Place fillets on the edge of a roasting rack. Cook on MEDIUM-HIGH (70–80%) for 10 minutes, turning once and basting.

❸ Stand for 5 minutes, covered with foil, to finish cooking.

❹ Drain off any juices from meat and mix with the marinade in an ovenable glass jug. Cook on HIGH (90–100%) for 1 minute.

❺ Dissolve cornflour in a little cold water and stir quickly into liquid. Cook for 20 seconds on HIGH (90–100%), stir and pour over diagonally sliced meat.

VARIATIONS

● Use cranberry sauce instead of plum sauce.
● Blend red wine with soy sauce and brown sugar for marinade.

EASY TIPS
For a richer coloured sauce do not add meat juice to the marinade when making the gravy.

Select similar sized fillets for even cooking results.

SERVING SUGGESTION

● Serve with One-Stir Green Fry (see page 87) and Fried Rice (see page 69).

VEAL AND MUSHROOM CASEROLE

Veal is lean, fine-grained meat and should always be tender. When cooking in the microwave, make sure you select good quality veal as leanness can sometimes produce tough results. Veal is more tender when cooked to well done.

500 g veal schnitzel
1 large onion, sliced
1 × 440 g can mushroom soup, lukewarm
¼ cup dry sherry
2 tablespoons sour cream
1 tablespoon freshly chopped herbs (parsley, coriander or chives)

METHOD
1. Lightly pound veal, pierce and cut into thin strips. Place in a large microware container.
2. Cook on MEDIUM–HIGH (70–80%) for 5 minutes, stirring once.
3. Soften onion in container lid, on HIGH (90–100%), for 1 minute covered with plastic wrap.
4. Stir soup and sherry into meat. Mix in blanched onion and cover container.
5. Cook on MEDIUM–HIGH (70–80%) for 5–6 minutes, stirring once.
6. Season to taste and stir in herbs and sour cream. Stand for 4 minutes, then serve.

VARIATION
- Add a small can of sliced mushrooms in butter sauce, for a richer finish.

SERVING SUGGESTION
- Serve with Steamed Rice (see page 67).

SERVES 4

PREPARATION TIME
8 minutes

COOKING TIME
16 minutes

UTENSIL
Large container (1.5 litre) and cover

ACCESSORY
Plastic wrap

EASY TIP
Use all-natural soups or salt-reduced varieties for best microwave results, as the speed of microwave cooking highlights flavours.

PASTA AND RICE

Microwave cooking times are about the same as conventional cooking times for these dry staples. However the finished texture of microwave-cooked rice and pasta is excellent and, of course, reheating them is a breeze as they reheat quickly and easily without drying or changing textures.

- Cook rice by the absorption method – where all water is absorbed by the rice – rather than in a large volume of water.
- Use a large enough container to allow boiling without spills.
- Slender noodles cook better in the microwave oven than the larger pasta shells.
- Add a teaspoon of oil or butter to the water. It will speed cooking of rice and pasta, and stop the latter sticking together.
- Salt can be added, if required, as there is sufficient fluid to prevent rice and pasta toughening.
- Do not cover rice during the first 10 minutes of cooking time, to prevent the water from boiling over the sides of the container.
- Do not completely cover pasta whilst cooking.
- Rice and pasta will not stick to the containers or burn in the microwave oven.
- At the end of cooking fork through rice and rinse pasta thoroughly. Serve from the cooking container for your convenience.
- Do not allow cooked pasta to stand in boiling water as it will overcook.
- If cooking large amounts of rice or pasta it is better to do so conventionally.

PASTA AND RICE COOKING GUIDE

Cook for the minimum time at first. It is easy to add extra cooking if necessary.

FOOD	TECHNIQUE	POWER	TIME
PASTA Slender pasta only	Use a 2 litre ovenable glass jug. Drop 250 g of slender pasta into 1.5 litres boiling water with 2 teaspoons oil. Half cover. Stir several times during cooking. Do not stand or pasta will overcook.	HIGH (90–100%)	For 250 g: 7–9 min.
RICE Quick brown	Put 1 cup rice, salt to taste, a knob of butter or drop of oil in 2 cups of lukewarm water in 1.5 litre container. Cook on HIGH at first, followed by MEDIUM. When water is all absorbed stir through and let stand before serving.	HIGH (90–100%) followed by MEDIUM (40–50%)	HIGH for 5 min., then MEDIUM for 20 min. + 3–5 min. standing time.
White, long-grain	Put 1 cup rice, salt to taste in 1¾ cups lukewarm water in 1.5 litre container. Cook uncovered until all water absorbed. Fork through. Stand covered before serving.	HIGH (90–100%)	10 min. + 3–4 min. standing time.

Note Standing time is approximately one-quarter of cooking time.

EASY MACARONI CHEESE

SERVES 4

PREPARATION TIME
6 minutes

COOKING TIME
15 minutes

UTENSIL
*Extra-large container
(2.25 litre)*

Easier dishes to cook are hard to find.

2 cups pasta (macaroni or spirals)
1 tablespoon oil
5 cups boiling water
1 cup White Sauce (see page 108)
2 cups grated cheese
freshly ground black pepper
chopped parsley for garnish

METHOD

❶ Place pasta and oil in boiling water in an extra-large container. Cook uncovered on HIGH (90–100%) for 10 minutes. Drain and rinse.

❷ Put sauce and cheese in the container and heat for 1 minute on MEDIUM (50–60%). Stir well.

❸ Add pasta and mix thoroughly.

❹ Cook on MEDIUM (50–60%) for 2–3 minutes until heated through.

❺ Season with black pepper and chopped parsley.

VARIATIONS

● Add 2 teaspoons mustard to White Sauce.

● Add chopped bacon or sliced salami to pasta and sauce.

SERVING SUGGESTION

● Serve with a green salad with vinaigrette dressing.

EASY TIP
*Pasta will cook on if
allowed to stand in boiling
water. Drain and run
water over it quickly.
Reheat as required.*

TANGY TOMATO AND PASTA SOUP

This is not a traditional tomato soup as the citrus flavour of the oranges adds bite to the tomatoes, while giving a little sweetness as well.

1 onion, chopped
1 × 810 g can crushed tomatoes
1 cup orange juice
1 cup hot tap water
1 × 85 g packet instant chicken noodles

METHOD

❶ Place onion in an extra-large container and cover. Cook, covered, to blanch on HIGH (90–100%) for 1 minute.

❷ Add tomatoes, orange juice and water. Cover and bring to the boil. Cook on HIGH (90–100%) for approximately 12–15 minutes, stirring occasionally.

❸ Add chicken flavouring from noodle sachet, stir well. Break up noodles and stir into soup.

❹ Cook on HIGH (90–100%) for a further 5 minutes, stirring once during cooking. Stand for 4 minutes.

VARIATION

● Add a cup of cooked rice in place of the noodles.

SERVING SUGGESTION

● Serve with crusty bread.

SERVES 6

PREPARATION TIME
3 minutes

COOKING TIME
24 minutes

UTENSIL
Extra-large container (2.25 litre)

EASY TIPS
To peel a tomato, prick the skin lightly with a fork, elevate on a roasting rack and heat for 45 seconds on HIGH (90–100%). Stand for 4 minutes, then peel.

To peel onions and avoid tears, trim ends of the onion. Place on a paper towel and microwave on HIGH (90–100%) for 1 minute. Remove the skin, then chop.

PASTA SEAFOOD TOSS

SERVES 6

PREPARATION TIME
2 minutes

COOKING TIME
12 minutes

UTENSIL
*Extra-large container
(2.25 litre)*

If you are looking for speed, ease and convenience, this is the perfect dish for you. Cold it makes a super summer salad.

2 cups spiral noodles
1 × 200 g tub sour cream
1 × 200 g can prawns, drained
1 avocado, diced
50 g flaked almonds, toasted

METHOD
1. Cook noodles in 5 cups boiling water on HIGH (90–100%) in extra-large container for 10 minutes.
2. Drain and immediately stir in sour cream.
3. Add prawns and avocado, toss well.
4. Cover, heat on MEDIUM (50–60%) for 2 minutes.
5. Stir in almonds just before serving.

VARIATIONS
● Add chopped herbs or lemon juice.
● Use a can of crabmeat or seafood marinara instead of prawns.

SERVING SUGGESTION
● Can be served cold as a salad. Either add sour cream to cold noodles or additional sour cream when cold.

EASY TIPS
Do not allow cooked pasta to stand in boiling water as it will cook on, resulting in overcooking.

Cook pasta uncovered to prevent water boiling over.

PUMPKIN LASAGNE

Everyone likes lasagne. Use your microwave oven to enjoy the colour, aroma and flavour of this tasty, non-traditional pumpkin lasagne.

8 sheets instant spinach lasagne noodles
1 quantity White Sauce (see page 108)
1 cup grated cheese
2 cups cooked pumpkin
250 g fresh ricotta cheese
1 egg
2 cloves garlic, crushed

METHOD
1. Stand lasagne sheets in 2–3 cups boiling water while preparing filling and sauce.
2. Make White Sauce as directed. Add cheese and stir to melt.
3. Purée pumpkin, ricotta, egg and garlic together. Season to taste.
4. Lay sheets of lasagne on base of a lightly oiled microware container.
5. Cover evenly with ⅓ of pumpkin mixture. Repeat these layers finishing with lasagne sheets.
6. Pour cheese sauce over. Cover and cook on MEDIUM–HIGH (70–80%) for 10–12 minutes. Stand for 4 minutes.

VARIATIONS
- Plain lasagne noodles can be used.
- Spread a layer of home-made Tomato Sauce (see page 109) in middle layer.
- Add some softened onion when puréeing vegetable mixture.

SERVING SUGGESTION
- Serve sprinkled with paprika or top with a little Tomato Sauce (see page 109).

SERVES 4

PREPARATION TIME
25 minutes

COOKING TIME
23 minutes

UTENSIL
25 cm square container (to fit 2 sheets of lasagne flat on bottom)

ACCESSORY
Plastic wrap

EASY TIPS
Cook 1 kg butternut pumpkin in its jacket: pierce skin several times, elevate on a roasting rack and cook on HIGH (90–100%) for 10–12 minutes. Stand to cool and then scoop out cooked purée. 1 kg butternut pumpkin cooked makes approximately 2 cups puréed pumpkin.

As you are unable to stir lasagne, place the dish on the edge of the turntable. Half-way through the cooking time push it to opposite side.

STEAMED RICE

SERVES 4

PREPARATION TIME
2 minutes

COOKING TIME
15 minutes

UTENSIL
*Extra-large container
(2.25 litres)*

It doesn't save much time to microwave rice but the texture is excellent. Also, rice doesn't stick or burn in the microwave oven. Add 1 tablespoon of butter or light oil to speed the cooking.

*1¾ cups lukewarm water
1 cup long-grain rice
1 tablespoon light oil*

METHOD
1 Place rice, oil and water in an extra-large container.
2 Cook uncovered on HIGH (90–100%) for 10–12 minutes until all water is absorbed and rice cooked. Fork through rice.
3 Stand, covered, for 3 minutes.

VARIATIONS
● Cook rice in stock instead of water for extra flavour.
● Toss through chopped fresh herbs when serving.

SERVING SUGGESTION
● Serve as a side dish with casseroles, stir frys, curries and roasts.

EASY TIP
Cooking rice uncovered prevents boilovers. If rice needs more cooking after 10 minutes, cover the container to speed the cooking, and cook for a further 2–3 minutes.

RISOTTO

This creamy Italian rice dish can be made in the microwave quite easily and without the constant attention and stirring it requires on the range top.

1 onion, finely chopped
30 g butter
1 cup rice
1 × 440 g can low-salt vegetable soup
1 cup grated cheese

METHOD

❶ Place onion and butter in the base of an extra-large container. Microwave on HIGH (90–100%) for 2 minutes.

❷ Add rice, stir well. Cook on HIGH (90–100%) for 2 minutes.

❸ Make soup up to 3 cups (750 ml) with hot water. Add to rice and stir through well.

❹ Cook uncovered on HIGH (90–100%) for 10 minutes. Stir and cook a further 10 minutes. Fork through rice.

❺ Sprinkle with cheese and stand, covered, for 1–2 minutes.

VARIATION

● Any vegetable soup may be used – such as pea, mushroom, tomato or pumpkin.

SERVING SUGGESTION

● Serve with crusty bread as a meal on its own or as an accompaniment to chicken or meat, especially veal.

SERVES 4

PREPARATION TIME
2 minutes

COOKING TIME
25 minutes

UTENSIL
Extra-large container
(2.25 litre)

EASY TIPS
Cooked rice can be stored in the refrigerator in an airtight container.

Always reheat rice with some water, stock, wine or butter in a covered dish in order to keep it moist.

FRIED RICE

SERVES 4

PREPARATION TIME
7 minutes

COOKING TIME
9 minutes

UTENSIL
Large container (1.5 litre)

ACCESSORY
Paper towel

EASY TIPS
Leftover steamed rice from the day before can be refrigerated overnight, or successfully frozen until needed.

Use frozen mixed vegetables for convenience or a combination of fresh spring onion, corn kernels, red pepper and bean shoots.

To blanch vegetables in the microwave oven, cut into bite-sized pieces. Place in a shallow dish. Cover tightly with plastic wrap. Cook on HIGH (90–100%) for 2 minutes. Add to casseroles, stir frys, soups and mornays.

You can't match rice for an inexpensive, nutritious and easy meal in one. For the health-conscious cook this is a tasty and simple recipe that cuts down on animal protein whilst increasing carbohydrate intake.

1 egg, beaten
2 rashers bacon, diced
30 g butter
1 cup Steamed Rice (see page 67)
½ cup blanched vegetables (for instance, celery, peas and capsicum)
1 teaspoon soy sauce.

METHOD
1. Pour well-beaten egg into a small shallow dish or lid. Cook on MEDIUM (50–60%) for 50–60 seconds.
2. Allow egg to stand for 1 minute. Remove and cut into thin strips.
3. Cook bacon between sheets of absorbent paper towel on HIGH (90–100%) for 1 minute.
4. Melt butter in the base of a large container for 40 seconds on HIGH (90–100%).
5. Add cooked rice, stir well to coat with butter. Mix in egg, bacon and vegetables.
6. Cook on HIGH (90–100%) for 4–5 minutes or until hot, stirring twice.
7. Pour soy sauce over rice and stir through. Stand 1 minute and serve.

VARIATIONS
● Use cooked diced pork instead of bacon, or drained canned prawns.
● Use brown rice.

SAVOURY RICE SLICE

Use brown rice to vary family meals, which
should be delicious as well as healthy and
simple. Rice slice is good hot or cold, and
quick brown rice has all the natural
goodness of brown rice whilst cooking in a
shorter time.

1 cup quick-cook brown rice
1 large carrot, grated
1 large zucchini, grated
1 × 300 g can tomato supreme (or flavoured
 canned tomatoes)
3 eggs
2 cloves garlic, crushed

METHOD
❶ Cook rice in 2 cups boiling water in
 microware container, uncovered, on HIGH
 (90–100%) for 15 minutes, until water is
 absorbed.
❷ Mix remaining ingredients together and
 stir thoroughly into rice.
❸ Cover, cook on MEDIUM–HIGH (70–80%) for
 8–10 minutes, until almost set in the
 centre.
❹ Stand for 5 minutes and then slice and
 serve.

VARIATIONS
● Sprinkle with grated cheddar or
 parmesan cheese and chopped herbs
 before standing.
● Use a can of baked beans in place of
 tomatoes.

SERVING SUGGESTIONS
● Serve with meat or chicken dishes.
● Serve on its own with salad.

SERVES 6

PREPARATION TIME
5 minutes

COOKING TIME
30 minutes

UTENSIL
Large container (1.5 litre)

EASY TIPS
*Add a teaspoon of oil or a
knob of butter to speed the
cooking process and
improve the texture of
brown rice.*

*Freeze leftover rice slices
then defrost and reheat as
required for healthy snacks.*

VEGETABLES

....

The microwave oven cooks fresh vegetables beautifully on HIGH (90–100%), in a shorter time than conventionally, without boiling out their natural goodness. This results in true flavours, colours and textures together with a better nutrient content.

- The best method of cooking each vegetable depends on its texture, shape and size. Cook vegetables that have their own protective jacket or cover with no water. Otherwise cook with minimum water and cover the dish.
- Always weigh trimmed vegetables, and then time accurately to achieve best results.
- Cut vegetables into uniform sizes so they cook evenly and quickly.
- Select the right size container to hold the vegetables comfortably.
- Use a microwave-safe freezer bag or oven bag if the right container is not available.
- Do not add salt to cooking water as it draws moisture from vegetables and toughens them.
- Allow for different sizes and densities when cooking a mixture of vegetables, ensuring the larger, fibrous vegetables, which take longer to cook, are placed around the outside of the container with small tender vegetables, that require shorter cooking, in the centre.
- Add herbs and spices, butter or lemon juice during cooking and season, if needed, after cooking.
- Stir vegetables during cooking time, especially those cooked in small, deep containers.
- Do not forget vegetables continue to 'cook on' during standing time.

● A good rule to follow when cooking several courses for a meal in the microwave oven is to cook the vegetables last so they remain crisp and colourful.

VEGETABLE COOKING GUIDE

All fresh vegetables should be cooked unsalted and covered, unless otherwise stated.

Defrosting information is given in this chart as defrosting frozen vegetables also involves cooking them. Home-grown and home-frozen vegetables will take longer to defrost and cook in the microwave than commercially frozen varieties. Place frozen vegetables in a shallow dish and cover. You do not need to add water. Stir or turn several times while defrosting.

VEGE-TABLE	TECHNIQUE	POWER	COOKING TIME (FRESH VEGE-TABLES)	DEFROST-ING/COOK-ING TIME (FROM FREEZER)
Artichoke, globe	Soak for 10 min. Remove coarse leaves, snip tips and stem.	HIGH (90–100%)	For 4 artichokes: 8–10 min. + standing time.	
Artichoke, Jerusalem	Peel and slice thinly. Add 1 tablespoon water.	HIGH (90–100%)	per 250 g: 8 min. + standing time.	
Asparagus	Trim ends and peel. Arrange as spokes of wheel, tips in centre. Add 1 tablespoon water.	HIGH (90–100%)	per 500 g: 4–6 min. + standing time.	per 250 g: 4–6 min. + standing time.
Bean sprouts	Rinse well and cook with rinse water only.	HIGH (90–100%)	per 250 g: 2 min. + standing time.	

Note Standing time is approximately one-quarter of cooking time.

VEGE-TABLE	TECHNIQUE	POWER	COOKING TIME (FRESH VEGE-TABLES)	DEFROST-ING/COOK-ING TIME (FROM FREEZER)
Beans, broad	Cook with ¼ cup water.	MEDIUM–HIGH (70–80%)	per 500 g: 6–8 min. + standing time.	per 250 g: 6–8 min. + standing time.
Beans, French	Remove string if necessary. Top and tail. Halve or slice lengthways. Arrange as spokes of wheel. Add ¼ cup water.	HIGH (90–100%)	per 500 g: 7–8 min. + standing time.	per 225 g: 6–8 min. + standing time.
Beetroot	Chose small beets. Trim stalks and wash well. Leave skin and roots on. Pierce with sharp knife.	HIGH (90–100%)	per 500 g: 10–12 min. + standing time.	
Broccoli	Trim stalks. Cut into florets. If stalks are thick cut cross in base. Arrange with stalks to outer edge. Add 1 tablespoon water.	HIGH (90–100%)	per 500 g: 5–6 min. + standing time.	per 225 g: 4–6 min. + standing time. per 500 g: 6–8 min. + standing time.
Brussels sprouts	Removed damaged leaves. Cut small cross in base. Add ¼ cup water.	HIGH (90–100%)	per 500 g: 8–10 min. + standing time.	
Cabbage	Remove damaged leaves. Finely shred into ribbons. Rinse and cook in rinse water only.	HIGH (90–100%)	per 500 g: 5–7 min. + standing time.	

Note Standing time is approximately one-quarter of cooking time.

VEGE-TABLE	TECHNIQUE	POWER	COOKING TIME (FRESH VEGE-TABLES)	DEFROST-ING/COOK-ING TIME (FROM FREEZER)
Cabbage, red	As **Cabbage**.	HIGH (90–100%)	per 500 g: 6–8 min. + stand-ing time.	
Capsicum	Thinly slice. Sauté, uncovered, with 30 g butter or ¼ cup stock.	HIGH (90–100%)	per 500 g: 4–6 min. + stand-ing time.	
Carrot	If young, scrape and leave whole. If older, peel and grate, slice or dice. Add 2 tablespoons water.	HIGH (90–100%)	per 250 g: 4–5 min. + stand-ing time.	per 250 g: 5–7 min. + stand-ing time. per 500g: 8–10 min. + stand-ing time.
Cauli-flower	Cut into florets. Add 2 table-spoons water.	HIGH (90–100%)	per 500 g: 6–8 min. + stand-ing time.	per 250 g: 5–6 min. + stand-ing time. per 500 g: 6–8 min. + stand-ing time.
Celery	Cut into 2 cm pieces. Add 1 tablespoon water and 1 tablespoon butter.	HIGH (90–100%)	per 500 g: 4–6 min. + stand-ing time.	
Corn, kernels	Remove from cob. Add 1 table-spoon water or butter.	HIGH (90–100%)	per 250 g: 4–6 min. + stand-ing time.	
Corn on the cob	Pull husk back and remove silk threads. Rub butter and spices over corn and re-cover with husk.	HIGH (90–100%)	per cob: 2–3 min. + stand-ing time.	

Note Standing time is approximately one-quarter of cooking time.

VEGE-TABLE	TECHNIQUE	POWER	COOKING TIME (FRESH VEGE-TABLES)	DEFROST-ING/COOK-ING TIME (FROM FREEZER)
Eggplant	Slice, unpeeled, in 1 cm slices. Cook with 2 tablespoons butter or stock.	HIGH (90–100%)	per 500 g: 6–8 min. + stand-ing time.	
Leek	Remove roots and tops. Wash well and slice lengthways. Add 2 tablespoons water.	HIGH (90–100%)	per 500 g: 6–8 min. + stand-ing time.	
Marrow	Peel if desired, remove seeds and slice. Add 1 tablespoon water and 1 tablespoon butter.	HIGH (90–100%)	per 250 g: 4 min. + standing time.	
Mush-room	Wipe with damp cloth. Leave whole or slice. Add 1 table-spoon butter.	HIGH (90–100%)	per 250 g: 2–3 min. + stand-ing time.	
Onion	Peel. Leave whole if small, cut in half or slice. Add 1–2 tablespoons water or butter.	HIGH (90–100%)	per 500 g: 4–7 min. + stand-ing time.	
Parsnip	Peel, slice or cut lengthways. Remove core from older pars-nips. Add 2 tablespoons water or 1 table-spoon butter.	HIGH (90–100%)	per 500 g: 6–8 min. + stand-ing time.	

Note Standing time is approximately one-quarter of cooking time.

VEGE-TABLE	TECHNIQUE	POWER	COOKING TIME (FRESH VEGE-TABLES)	DEFROST-ING/COOK-ING TIME (FROM FREEZER)
Peas	Shell. Add 1 tablespoon water and 1 tablespoon castor sugar.	HIGH (90–100%)	per 500 g: 4–6 min. + standing time.	per 500 g: 4–6 min. + standing time.
Potato	New: wash, scrape and cube. Old: peel. Cook in rinse water with squeeze of lemon juice.	HIGH (90–100%)	per 500 g: 8–10 min. + standing time.	
Potato, baked	Wash well. Prick skin. Turn once during cooking.	HIGH (90–100%)	3–4 min. per medium potato + standing time.	
Pumpkin	Butternut: pierce skin in several places. Cook on roasting rack. Turn once during cooking. Large pumpkins: cut into wedges. Remove seeds and skin. Add 2 tablespoons water.	HIGH (90–100%)	Butternut, per 500 g: 7–8 min. + standing time. Large pumpkins, per 500 g: 8 min. + standing time.	
Silver beet	Wash well. Remove coarse stem. Cut into wide ribbons. Cook with rinse water.	HIGH (90–100%)	per 500 g: 5–7 min.+ standing time.	
Snow peas	Trim, string and rinse well. Cook with rinse water only.	HIGH (90–100%)	per 500 g: 3–4 min. **Do not stand**.	

Note Standing time is approximately one-quarter of cooking time.

VEGE-TABLE	TECHNIQUE	POWER	COOKING TIME (FRESH VEGE-TABLES)	DEFROST-ING/COOK-ING TIME (FROM FREEZER)
Spinach	Wash well. Cook with rinse water only.	HIGH (90–100%)	per 250 g: 2–3 min. + standing time.	per 250 g: 6–7 min. + standing time.
Swede	Peel and cut into thin slices. Add ⅓ cup water.	HIGH (90–100%)	per 500 g: 12–14 min. + standing time.	
Sweet potato	Wash, peel and cut into 4 cm rounds. Add ¼ cup water.	HIGH (90–100%)	per 500 g: 8–10 min. + standing time.	
Tomato	Halve. Cook with rinse water only.	HIGH (90–100%)	per 500 g: 4–5 min. + standing time.	
Turnip	If large, peel and dice. If small, cook whole. Add 2 tablespoons water.	HIGH (90–100%)	per 500 g: 6–8 min. + standing time.	
Witloof	Remove portion of bitter core. Sprinkle with lemon juice. Arrange on dish with thicker base facing out. Add 1–2 tablespoons stock or water.	HIGH (90–100%)	per 500 g: 6–8 min. + standing time.	
Zucchini	If small, trim ends and leave whole. If large, cut in half lengthways, slice into strips or grate. Add 1 tablespoon butter or water.	HIGH (90–100%)	per 250 g: 3–4 min. + standing time.	

Note Standing time is approximately one-quarter of cooking time.

VEGETABLE MEDLEY

Cook three vegetables all at once on a plain dinner plate so they can go from the oven to table for easy serving.

250 g baby potatoes (about 6), cleaned and rinsed
250 g pumpkin, cut into 4 x 1 cm sticks
1 cup frozen peas
30 g butter, melted
1 tablespoon chives, finely chopped
1 tablespoon parsley, finely chopped
freshly ground black pepper

METHOD
1. Pierce potato skins and arrange potatoes on the edge of plate.
2. Make a circle of the pumpkin sticks inside the potatoes.
3. Place peas in the centre of the plate.
4. Mix herbs with melted butter and drizzle over the vegetables.
5. Season with pepper and cover with plastic wrap.
6. Cook on HIGH (90–100%) for 8 minutes.
7. Allow to stand for 1–3 minutes to finish cooking.

VARIATION
- Use cauliflower florets, carrot sticks and zucchini rounds.

SERVING SUGGESTION
- Serve with Roast Chicken (see page 43), Lamb Racks (see page 57) or Meatloaf Made Easy (see page 53).

SERVES 4

PREPARATION TIME
6 minutes

COOKING TIME
9–11 minutes

UTENSIL
1 plain 20–25 cm round dinner plate

ACCESSORY
Plastic wrap

EASY TIPS
Place a whole pumpkin in the microwave and cook on HIGH (90–100%) *for 2–4 minutes to make it easy to cut.*

Always place the stems of vegetables like cauliflower and broccoli to the outside of the dish so they cook evenly, as the stems are tougher than the flowers.

TOMATO AND ONION PIE

SERVES 4

PREPARATION TIME
5 minutes

COOKING TIME
7 minutes

UTENSIL
Medium container (1 litre)

Good tomatoes are available in Australia for most of the year. Combined with onion and a green vegetable they make a flavoursome and colourful pie in mere minutes.

2 large firm tomatoes
1 small onion, grated
¼ green capsicum, finely sliced
pepper and salt to taste
parmesan cheese for dusting

METHOD
1. Cut tomatoes with a serrated knife into 1 cm slices.
2. Place half the tomatoes in the base of a medium microware container and season.
3. Sprinkle with grated onion and cover with green capsicum.
4. Top with the other half of the tomato slices, season, dust with cheese and cover the container.
5. Place off the centre of the turntable and cook on HIGH (90–100%) for 5 minutes, moving the dish to the opposite side of the turntable at the half-way point.
6. Stand several minutes before slicing and serving.

VARIATION
● 1 small, finely sliced zucchini or a finely sliced celery stick, to replace the green capsicum.

SERVING SUGGESTION
● Serve with a roast, barbecue or grill.

EASY TIPS
To peel a tomato, prick the skin lightly with a fork, elevate on a roasting rack and heat for 45 seconds on HIGH (90–100%). Stand for 5 minutes, then peel.

Tomatoes are best stored at room temperature in a dry, airy spot. Refrigeration destroys their flavour and texture.

CITRUS CARROTS

The lively colour and natural sweetness of fresh carrots are highlighted when they are prepared and cooked properly in the microwave.

3 carrots, cut into sticks 3 cm long × 1 cm across
50 ml chicken or vegetable stock
juice of 2 oranges
1 teaspoon honey
1 tablespoon fresh basil, finely chopped

METHOD

❶ Combine stock, orange juice and honey in jug and heat on HIGH (90–100%) for 1 minute to blend.

❷ Place carrot sticks in a spoke-wheel configuration around the base of microware container and pour stock mixture over.

❸ Sprinkle with basil and cover the container.

❹ Place the dish off the centre of the turntable and cook on HIGH (90–100%) for 5 minutes.

❺ Stand 1½ minutes before removing carrots with a slotted spoon and serving.

VARIATION

● Cook with 60 g melted butter and 1 tablespoon fresh rosemary. Garnish with orange rind.

SERVING SUGGESTIONS

● Serve garnished with ¼ cup seedless green grapes, when in season.
● Serve with Pork Fillets (see page 59).

SERVES 4

PREPARATION TIME
5 minutes

COOKING TIME
7–8 minutes

UTENSILS
Large container (1.5 litre)
500 ml ovenable glass jug

EASY TIP
Always keep the container covered when cooking vegetables as this traps the steam, shortens the cooking time and prevents the vegetables drying out.

SCALLOPED POTATOES

SERVES 4

PREPARATION TIME
3 minutes

COOKING TIME
22 minutes

UTENSIL
Roasting rack
Large container (1.5 litre)

ACCESSORY
Paper towel

EASY TIPS
For fast sautéd potatoes,
cut microwave-baked
potatoes in thick slices then
brown them quickly in
butter on top of the range.
Skins can be removed after
baking or left on.

For potato splits, slit the
top of the baked potato,
push in the ends to make a
pocket and fluff up the
potato. Add the topping of
your choice then reheat a
further minute in the
microwave to heat the
topping.

Potatoes can form the basis of a number of mouthwatering recipes, such as creamy mashed potatoes, stuffed potatoes or this ever-popular scalloped potatoes.

4 evenly sized potatoes (about 600 g), washed
and scrubbed
2 tablespoons chopped spring onions
300 ml White Sauce (see page 108) seasoned with
½ teaspoon mustard
paprika for dusting
salt and black pepper to taste

METHOD
1. Prick potatoes all over with a fork.
2. Arrange around the edge of a roasting rack or place on paper towel around the rim of the turntable.
3. Cook on HIGH (90–100%) for 8 minutes, turning over once.
4. Allow to stand, wrapped in a towelling tea towel, to complete cooking.
5. Peel cooked potatoes and slice in 5 mm slices. Circle potato slices around base of the microware container. Sprinkle with spring onions and season.
6. Pour over white sauce, dust with paprika, cover and heat through positioned off the centre of the turntable for 5 minutes on MEDIUM-HIGH (70–80%), moving container to the opposite side of the turntable half-way through cooking time.
7. Stand 1 minute before serving.

VARIATION
● Add cooked, diced bacon and garnish with grated tasty cheese.

COLOURFUL CAULIFLOWER AU GRATIN

Cauliflower cooks quickly and easily in the microwave oven without creating a smell in the kitchen.

250 g cauliflower florets, rinsed
150 g broccoli florets, rinsed
1 cup White Sauce (see page 108)
½ cup parmesan cheese
paprika for dusting

SERVES 4

PREPARATION TIME
5 minutes

COOKING TIME
19 minutes

UTENSIL
Large container (1.5 litre)

METHOD

❶ Place cauliflower around the outer edge of microware container.

❷ Place broccoli florets in the centre of the container, cover dish and place off the centre of the turntable.

❸ Cook on HIGH (90–100%) for 7 minutes, moving the dish to the opposite side of the turntable at the half-way point.

❹ Remove from the oven and drain moisture from vegetables into the white sauce.

❺ Stir in cheese and reheat sauce on MEDIUM-HIGH (70–80%) for 1 minute to blend.

❻ Pour sauce over vegetables. Sprinkle with paprika and cook for 3 minutes on HIGH (90–100%). Stand 1 minute before serving.

VARIATIONS

● Mustard may be added to white sauce if cooking cauliflower on its own.
● Add sliced salami or cabana for a spicy flavour.

EASY TIPS
Cut fresh vegetables for microwaving into uniform sizes so they cook evenly.

Arrange more tender vegetables in the middle of the container, as foods in the centre cook more slowly than those around the outside.

BUTTERNUT PUMPKIN PURÉE

SERVES 4

PREPARATION TIME
2 minutes

COOKING TIME
20 minutes

UTENSIL
Roasting rack

Cooked in its jacket, pumpkin (a member of the squash family) can be turned into a purée, made into soup, added to damper or scones or cooked as a sweet pie. The most popular pumpkin is the Queensland Blue which has a thick, greeny-blue skin. Heating it in the microwave for 2–3 minutes on HIGH (90–100%) makes it easy to cut up. Here, however, is a recipe for the smaller, orange-skinned butternut.

1 butternut pumpkin (approximately 1 kg)
¼ cup cream
salt and black pepper to taste
1 tablespoon finely chopped chives

METHOD
1. Pierce pumpkin skin well all over.
2. Elevate pumpkin on a roasting rack with narrow part towards the centre.
3. Cook on HIGH (90–100%) for 15 minutes, turning over once.
4. Stand for 5 minutes.
5. Cut in half, remove seeds, scoop out flesh.
6. Blend flesh with cream, season and serve garnished with chives.

VARIATIONS
- Allow 10 minutes only cooking time for firmer pumpkin that can then be cut into sticks or diced for a salad.
- Toss with French dressing or mix with yoghurt and finely chopped mint.

EASY TIPS
If preferred, the whole pumpkin can be heated just long enough to cut it in half. Remove the stringy centre and seeds then microwave the halved pumpkin until it's as tender as you want for the recipe.

If cooked long enough pumpkin gets mushy and falls off the rind.

ZUCCHINI AND CORN SLICE

This slice is quick to prepare and easy to cook. Serve it warm with salad or chill and serve it cold as a barbecue or picnic dish.

1 tablespoon light oil
2 leeks, sliced
1 cup grated zucchini
1 × 220 g can corn kernels, well drained
freshly ground black pepper
300 ml cream
2 eggs, beaten
1 cup tasty cheese, grated
1 teaspoon paprika for dusting

METHOD

1. Place oil and leeks in the base of a large microwave container and cook on HIGH (90–100%) for 2 minutes.
2. Add zucchini, corn and pepper and mix in well with a spoonwhisk.
3. Beat eggs and cream together to combine. Stir in grated cheese.
4. Pour over vegetables. Sprinkle with paprika and cover container.
5. Place off the centre of the turntable and cook on MEDIUM-HIGH (70–80%) for 11 minutes, moving the dish to the opposite side of the turntable half-way through cooking.
6. Stand 4–5 minutes to ensure the centre has set before slicing.

VARIATIONS

- Add ¼ cup shredded cooked chicken or diced cooked bacon.
- Use sour cream in place of cream.

SERVES 4

PREPARATION TIME
5 minutes

COOKING TIME
18 minutes

UTENSIL
Large container (1.5 litre)

ACCESSORY
Spoonwhisk

EASY TIP
Cream microwaves well but will curdle when heated too quickly. It is advisable to microwave cream on MEDIUM-HIGH (70–80%) or MEDIUM (50–60%).

FRESH GREEN BEANS

SERVES 2–4

PREPARATION TIME
3 minutes

COOKING TIME
5 minutes

UTENSIL
Ovenable glass jug

ACCESSORY
Microwave-safe oven or freezer bag

Cooking times vary for green beans – the fresher and smaller the beans, the faster they cook in the microwave. Test beans after the minimum cooking time recommended.

1 tablespoon butter
juice of 1 lemon
freshly ground black pepper
250 g stringless green beans, topped and tailed

METHOD

❶ Melt butter in ovenable glass jug on HIGH (90–100%) for 30 seconds. Add lemon juice and black pepper to taste.
❷ Rinse beans and place in a microwave-safe plastic bag to form a single layer. Drizzle over melted butter and lemon juice mix.
❸ Knot the bag and place in the centre of the turntable.
❹ Microwave for 3½–4 minutes on HIGH (90–100%), turning over once.
❺ Stand for 1 minute and serve hot.

VARIATION

● After cooking drain and toss in French dressing. Serve cold.

SERVING SUGGESTION

● Serve with Roast Chicken (see page 43) or Pork Fillets (see page 59).

EASY TIPS
If beans are stringy, slice lengthways to cook. Beans require a little more water than most greens to cook well.

Do not salt, as salt dehydrates vegetables.

STUFFED TOMATOES

It's a pleasure to cook stuffed tomatoes in the microwave as they retain their shape and colour and do not collapse unless they are overcooked.

4 large firm tomatoes
½ cup cooked brown rice
¼ cup grated parmesan cheese
1 tablespoon chopped fresh basil
chilli sauce to taste

METHOD

❶ Remove cores from tomatoes. Scoop out flesh, taking care not to break skin of tomato.

❷ Mix tomato pulp, rice, cheese, basil and dash of chilli sauce together.

❸ Fill cavity of tomatoes with mixture. Arrange tomatoes around edge of large microware container. Cover with paper towel.

❹ Cook on HIGH (90–100%) for 4 minutes. Stand 1 minute before serving.

VARIATIONS

● Use mozzarella or cheddar cheese.
● Add salami to rice stuffing.

SERVING SUGGESTION

● Serve with fish or as a great snack meal with a slice of bacon.

SERVES 4

PREPARATION TIME
15 minutes

COOKING TIME
5 minutes

UTENSIL
Large container (1.5 litre)

ACCESSORY
Paper towel

EASY TIP
For tomatoes, potatoes and other vegetables which have their own skin, cook where possible without water to improve the retention of nutrients.

ONE-STIR GREEN FRY

SERVES 4

PREPARATION TIME
10 minutes

COOKING TIME
4–5 minutes

UTENSIL
Medium container (1 litre)

ACCESSORY
Plastic wrap

Stir frys are ideal for the microwave as vegetables cut in the Chinese manner are uniform in size and colourful and crunchy at the finish. Mix and match an endless variety of vegetables as the seasons dictate.

½ green capsicum
1 stick celery
100 g broccoli
6 asparagus spears
40 g snow peas
freshly ground black pepper

METHOD

❶ Cut capsicum into 1 cm squares, slice celery into 5 mm pieces, break broccoli into small florets, cut asparagus into 2 cm pieces and top and tail snow peas.

❷ Arrange capsicum, celery and broccoli around edge of shallow microware container or its cover. Place snow peas and asparagus in the centre.

❸ Sprinkle with a little water and cover with vented plastic wrap.

❹ Microwave on HIGH (90–100%) for 3 minutes for a crunchy finish or 4–5 minutes for a softer finish. Stand 1 minute.

❺ Toss vegetables and season with ground black pepper.

EASY TIPS
Remember to use a minimum amount of water when cooking vegetables as most vegetables cook in their own natural water, thereby retaining maximum nutritional value.

Never add salt before microwave cooking vegetables as this leaches out their moisture.

VARIATIONS

● Any green vegetables may be used, e.g. zucchini, beans, cabbage.

● Toss through toasted pine kernels or flaked almonds.

● Add a squeeze of lemon juice.

BREAD AND CAKES

Cake and bread cooking is easy in the microwave oven. The most important thing to remember when cooking cakes in the microwave is not to overcook, so they remain moist. Microwaved cakes do not brown as they do when conventionally cooked so they need decorating.

Breads are porous and for this reason they cook very fast, so do not have time to dry and form a crust. They too need dusting with spice or decorating with seeds to enhance their appearance.

- Cook most breads uncovered to prevent them from becoming soggy.
- Let cake batter rest for 10 minutes before cooking to ensure an even finish. Pass a knife through the batter several times to release air before pouring into the pan and cooking.
- Line the bottom of your ring dish with paper towel to absorb excess moisture and provide a smooth surface for icing cakes.
- Do not fill cake containers more than half full because of the expansion that occurs when microwave cooking.
- Elevate cakes when cooking, so microwaves can pass underneath the container.
- Move cakes in the microwave oven for even cooking; opening and shutting the oven door will not make a microwave cake fall.
- Allow cakes to stand for the recommended standing time to finish cooking, then loosen the edges with a knife for easy removal.
- Because there is no crust on a microwave-baked cake you should ice, cover with plastic wrap or refrigerate, for maximum freshness.
- Do not overcook cakes; always follow the directions carefully and use the recommended container.

BANANA CAKE

SERVES 8

PREPARATION TIME
5 minutes

COOKING TIME
10 minutes

UTENSILS
Jug
Ring pan
Roasting rack

ACCESSORY
Paper towel

Bananas are one of the world's oldest known fruit. In Australia the banana is the third most popular fruit. The ubiquitous banana softens easily and maintains a superior flavour when microwaved.

1 cup brown sugar
¼ cup vegetable oil
3 ripe bananas, mashed
1 egg, beaten
1¼ cups self-raising flour
cinnamon sugar

METHOD

❶ Mix sugar and oil in a jug. Add mashed banana and egg, stir well.
❷ Add flour, mix with a fork until combined.
❸ Pour into a paper towel–lined ring pan.
❹ Elevate on rack, cook on HIGH (90–100%) for 5 minutes.
❺ Stand container directly on the bench, covered with paper towel, for 5 minutes.
❻ Turn cake out and sprinkle with cinnamon sugar.

VARIATION

● Add ¼ cup of chopped walnuts to batter.

SERVING SUGGESTIONS

● Serve warm or cold, sliced and buttered.
● Ice with a cream-cheese icing and dust with cinnamon.

EASY TIP
Allow cake to cool covered with a tea towel or paper towel, to keep the moisture in whilst preventing steaming.

HOME-MADE CHOCOLATE CAKE

Microwave-baked cakes are moist and tender if not overcooked. Because they do not brown during cooking, chocolate cake is an ideal cake to bake.

125 g butter
¾ cup brown sugar
⅓ cup cocoa
2 eggs
½ cup water or sour cream
1 cup self-raising flour

METHOD

❶ Melt butter in an ovenable glass jug on HIGH (90–100%) for approximately 40 seconds.

❷ Add sugar and cocoa, stir with a fork to dissolve any lumps.

❸ Add eggs, water or sour cream and flour, stir until just combined.

❹ Pour into a paper towel–lined ring pan.

❺ Cook, elevated on rack, on HIGH (90–100%) for 5 minutes.

❻ Stand covered with paper towel directly on the bench for 5 minutes. Turn out to cool completely before topping with chocolate icing.

VARIATIONS

● Add 1 teaspoon mixed spice with the cocoa.

● Use orange juice instead of water and top with orange icing.

SERVING SUGGESTION

● Serve warm with Custard (see page 115) or Handy Chocolate Sauce (see page 114) as a dessert.

SERVES 6–8

PREPARATION TIME
5 minutes

COOKING TIME
10 minutes

UTENSILS
Jug
Ring pan
Roasting rack

ACCESSORY
Paper towel

EASY TIPS
Mix ingredients with a fork only until just combined. Overbeating will cause cakes to dry out.

Cake is ready when a little of surface will remove when touched with a finger, and underneath is cooked.

Using sour cream results in a moist, finer-textured cake.

FUDGE BROWNIES

MAKES 24 PIECES

PREPARATION TIME
5 minutes

COOKING TIME
13 minutes

UTENSILS
27 × 17 cm oval dish
4 cup ovenable glass jug

Brownies are always popular and extremely easy to make.

200 g dark cooking chocolate, in small pieces
125 g butter
1 cup brown sugar
2 eggs, lightly beaten
1 cup self-raising flour
1 cup shredded coconut
¾ cup chopped walnuts
sifted icing sugar as topping

METHOD
1. Melt chocolate and butter together in glass jug on MEDIUM (50–60%) for 3–4 minutes.
2. Add sugar and eggs. Whisk with a fork. Add flour, mix well. Stir in coconut and walnuts.
3. Pour into an oval dish. Cook on MEDIUM-HIGH (70–80%) for 9–10 minutes on the edge of the turntable, moving to opposite side half-way through cooking time.
4. Leave in dish to finish cooking and cool completely.
5. Sprinkle with sifted icing sugar before cutting into pieces.

VARIATIONS
- Use pecan nuts, macadamia nuts or almonds instead of walnuts.
- Add chopped white or milk chocolate with the coconut.

SERVING SUGGESTION
- Serve warm with vanilla ice-cream or Custard (see page 115).

EASY TIPS
Use good quality cooking chocolate and not compounded chocolate.

Break chocolate into pieces for speedy melting.

Never melt chocolate covered, as it will stiffen.

UPSIDE-DOWN CAKE

This self-decorating cake cooks best in a
ring-shaped microware container.

Topping
50 g butter
2 tablespoons brown sugar
1 × 225 g can sliced pineapple
8 glacé cherries
Cake
125 g butter
¾ cup brown sugar
2 eggs, beaten
1 teaspoon ground ginger
1½ cups self-raising flour

METHOD
Topping
❶ Melt the butter in the ring pan on HIGH
(90–100%) for approximately 30 seconds.
❷ Add the sugar and stir to dissolve.
Spread evenly around base of ring pan.
❸ Drain pineapple, reserving juice. Cut
each slice in half and arrange on top of
caramelised sugar. Place a cherry in the
hollow of each pineapple.
Cake
❶ Melt butter in ovenable glass jug on
HIGH (90–100%) for about 1 minute.
❷ Add sugar, mix well. Add eggs.
❸ Make up reserved pineapple juice to ½
cup with water. Add to mixture, mix well.
❹ Add ginger and sift in flour, stir with a
fork until combined.
❺ Pour over fruit topping in pan base.
❻ Elevate on rack and cook off the centre
of turntable on MEDIUM-HIGH (70–80%) for
10 minutes, moving to the opposite side
half-way through cooking. Stand,
covered with paper towel, for 10 minutes
before turning onto a serving plate.

SERVES 6–8

PREPARATION TIME
10 minutes

COOKING TIME
22 minutes

UTENSILS
Ring pan
4 cup ovenable glass jug
Roasting rack

ACCESSORY
Paper towel

EASY TIP
*Soften hardened brown
sugar by placing in a
small microware container.
Add a wedge of apple,
cover and heat on HIGH
(90–100%) for 30–40
seconds. Stand for 30
seconds, remove apple and
stir sugar through.*

FRUIT MEDLEY PACKET CAKE

SERVES 6–8

PREPARATION TIME
5 minutes

COOKING TIME
11 minutes

UTENSILS
Ring pan
Roasting rack

ACCESSORY
Paper towel

EASY TIPS
Cook for 6 minutes in lower-wattage ovens.

Turn a packet cake into an old-fashioned trifle. Spread cake fingers thickly with jam and place in a glass serving dish. Sprinkle with sherry, top with canned fruit and pour over custard. Finish with a layer of cubed, ready-made jelly and refrigerate several hours before serving.

Microwave-cooked packet cakes are light and fluffy if not overcooked. You can prepare, cook and decorate these cakes in under 20 minutes.

1 × 310 g packet madeira or butter cake mix
½ teaspoon mixed spice
1 egg, lightly beaten
¾ cup apricot nectar
1 × 200 g packet fruit medley (chopped, dried fruit – peaches, pears, apricots, apples, sultanas)
vanilla sugar and mixed spice for dusting

METHOD

1 Mix cake mix and spice together. Add egg and apricot nectar. Stir with a fork until well combined. Fold in fruit medley.

2 Pour batter into ring pan lined with paper towel. Cook, elevated on rack, on HIGH (90–100%) for 5½ minutes in the centre of the turntable.

3 Stand directly on bench, covered with tea towel, for 5 minutes.

4 Turn out to cool. Dust with vanilla sugar and mixed spice.

VARIATIONS

● Use ground ginger rather than mixed spice.
● Use any flavoured fruit juice instead of nectar.
● Use ½ cup of pumpkin purée rather than fruit medley and only ½ cup liquid.

SERVING SUGGESTION

● Top with a cream-cheese icing. Decorate with extra mixed spice and cinnamon.

CORN DAMPER

This easy-bake damper is especially delicious as an accompaniment to a barbecue. The addition of golden corn and a pinch of cayenne pepper gives a lift to the taste of traditional damper.

1½ cups self-raising flour
½ teaspoon baking powder
¼–½ teaspoon cayenne pepper
1 tablespoon butter
1 × 130 g can creamed corn
⅓ cup milk
poppy or sesame seeds for topping

METHOD

❶ Sift flour, baking powder and cayenne pepper into a large mixing bowl. Rub in butter with fingertips.
❷ Make a well in the centre of dry ingredients. Pour milk and corn into the hollow. Mix thoroughly into the flour to make a soft dough.
❸ Press dough into a 25 cm round. Place on a roasting rack. Mark into six wedges. Brush with a little extra milk and sprinkle with poppy or sesame seeds.
❹ Place the rack off the centre of the turntable and cook on HIGH (90–100%) for 5 minutes, moving the damper from one side of the turntable to the other half-way through cooking time.
❺ Stand for 5 minutes before slicing.

VARIATIONS

● Use mashed pumpkin instead of corn.
● Add some grated, softened onion with corn.

SERVES 6

PREPARATION TIME
10 minutes

COOKING TIME
10 minutes

UTENSIL
Roasting rack

EASY TIP
Stand damper in a towelling tea towel to complete the on-going cooking process and prevent steaming. This way it will stay warm without becoming soggy.

TWO-TONE ANZAC BISCUITS

MAKES 30

PREPARATION TIME
15 minutes

COOKING TIME
30 minutes

UTENSILS
*4-cup ovenable glass jug
Roasting rack*

ACCESSORY
Baking paper

EASY TIP
*Chilling biscuit dough for
30 minutes before
microwaving produces a
crisper biscuit.*

Biscuits are tricky to make in the microwave. However, our own Aussie Anzac biscuits do cook successfully in the oven.

*125 g butter
2 tablespoons boiling water
1 tablespoon golden syrup
1 teaspoon bicarbonate of soda
1 cup flour
2 cups rolled oats
½ cup sugar*

METHOD
1 Melt butter in jug on HIGH (90–100%) for approximately 45 seconds.
2 Mix golden syrup and bicarbonate of soda in water. When bubbling, add to butter and mix well. Stir in flour, oats and sugar. Mix thoroughly.
3 Cover the flat back of a roasting rack with baking paper. Roll heaped teaspoons of mixture into balls. Place 6 evenly around edge of rack, allowing at least 3 cm between each.
4 Cook on MEDIUM-HIGH (70–80%) for 3 minutes or until biscuits turn a rich brown in the centre.
5 Stand for 2 minutes before removing to a wire rack to cool. Repeat procedure with remaining mixture.

SERVING SUGGESTION
● Serve with coffee or tea.

FAMILY SPONGE

This three-minute sponge will rise to the occasion every time if you remember to make sure that your eggs are *fresh and at room temperature* before beating.

½ cup self-raising flour
1 teaspoon each cinnamon, ground ginger, cocoa
3 eggs, separated
⅔ cup sugar

❶ Sift flour, spices and cocoa together twice into a bowl.
❷ Beat egg whites until stiff in another bowl. Gradually add sugar, beating well between additions.
❸ Add yolks to egg white mixture and beat until just mixed.
❹ Gently fold in flour mixture.
❺ Pour batter into a large microware container lined with paper towel. Cover and elevate on a roasting rack off the centre of the turntable.
❻ Cook on HIGH (90–100%) for 3 minutes, moving the rack and the container to the opposite side of the turntable half-way through the cooking time.
❼ Stand, covered with paper towel, for 3 minutes.
❽ Turn out and cool completely.

VARIATION
● For a plain sponge, omit spice and cocoa and add 1 tablespoon plain flour.

SERVING SUGGESTION
● Top with cream and fresh berries in season.

SERVES 4–6

PREPARATION TIME
10 minutes

COOKING TIME
6 minutes

UTENSILS
Large container (1.5 litre)
Roasting rack

ACCESSORY
Paper towel

EASY TIP
This sponge will be approximately 4 cm high. For a double sponge filled with cream you will need to make two cakes.

FAST-BAKE FRUIT CAKE

SERVES 10–12

PREPARATION TIME
25 minutes

COOKING TIME
45 minutes

UTENSILS
*Extra-large microware
container (2.25 litre)
22 cm round container
Roasting rack*

ACCESSORY
Paper towel

300 g each sultanas, raisins and currants
200 g glacé cherries, halved
½ cup brandy
250 g butter, softened
250 g dark brown sugar
4 eggs, at room temperature
1 teaspoon vanilla essence
350 g self-raising flour
2 teaspoons mixed spice
walnuts or pecan nuts for decoration

METHOD

❶ Mix together all fruits and brandy.

❷ Cook on HIGH (90–100%) for 7 minutes to plump fruit. Set aside to cool.

❸ In large microware container soften butter on LOW (30–40%) for 3 minutes. Add sugar, beat until light and fluffy.

❹ Add eggs, one at a time, then vanilla essence, beating well after each addition.

❺ Mix flour and spice. Add fruit and flour mixtures alternately to the creamed mixture, mixing thoroughly.

❻ Lightly grease a 22 cm round microwave container with extra light olive oil and line base with paper towel. Pour in mixture, smoothing surface.

❼ Arrange nuts over surface of the cake.

❽ Elevate cake on roasting rack, covered loosely with paper towel. Cook on DEFROST (30–35%) for 30–35 minutes off the centre of the turntable. Move cake to opposite side of turntable every 10 minutes.

❾ Cake is ready when a skewer inserted into centre comes out clean. Stand in container until cold. Invert on to plate. Remove paper towel. Turn back over and store in an airtight container.

EASY TIP
*For a darker cake add 1
tablespoon Parisian
Essence.*

DESSERTS

Desserts are easy to make in the microwave oven, be they puddings, fruits, custards or cheesecake. There are many advantages – a huge saving in time, savings in electricity costs and, of course, you and your kitchen remain cool.

- Include puddings on your microwave menu as they cook very evenly as microwave energy heats all their surfaces.
- Rotate or move puddings across the turntable to ensure both sides cook evenly when it is not possible to stir them.
- Elevate desserts on a roasting rack (or upturned saucer) for more even cooking.
- Do not peel fruit for baking, as fruit with the skin on maintains maximum nutrients, whilst retaining its shape.
- Reduce or eliminate sugar in recipes as some fruits that need sweetening when conventionally cooked do not need it when microwaved.
- Do not overcook fresh fruits as they are best served crisp-tender.
- Ensure all ingredients for baked custards are at room temperature. They will then cook and set best.
- Bake and serve cheesecake from one dish. Should you wish to remove it from the pie plate or dish, line the container with plastic wrap leaving 4 cm hanging over the edge of the dish to enable you to conveniently lift the cake from the dish.
- Desserts are easy to reheat – heat on HIGH (90–100%) for 30–60 seconds for 1 serving, or MEDIUM (50–60%) for 1–3 minutes for whole desserts.

SELF-SAUCING CHOCOLATE PUDDING

SERVES 6

PREPARATION TIME
7 minutes

COOKING TIME
8 minutes

UTENSILS
*Large container (1.5 litre)
Roasting rack*

A light, cake-style pudding that separates to self-sauce on the bottom whilst cooking.

*50 g butter
1 cup castor sugar
1 egg
½ cup milk
1 cup self-raising flour
2½ tablespoons cocoa
1¼ cups boiling water*

METHOD

1. Melt butter in a large microware container on HIGH (90–100%) for approximately 40 seconds.
2. Add ½ cup sugar, stir well. Add egg and milk and mix thoroughly.
3. Stir in flour and 1½ tablespoons cocoa. Mix with a fork until combined.
4. Mix remaining sugar and cocoa together and sprinkle over mixture in container.
5. Pour over boiling water.
6. Cook on HIGH (90–100%), uncovered, elevated on a roasting rack in the centre of the turntable for 5 minutes.
7. Stand for 2 minutes then serve straight from container.

VARIATION

- Butterscotch Pudding: omit cocoa and ½ cup sugar from topping; instead add 2 tablespoons golden syrup and 1 tablespoon butter to boiling water.

SERVING SUGGESTION

- Serve dusted with icing sugar and whipped cream.

EASY TIP
Microwave puddings and cakes have more volume than conventionally cooked ones. Fill containers no more than half full, to allow for the expansion that occurs.

LEMON PUDDING

The lemon is a valuable fruit in the kitchen as it enhances the flavour of many foods. It is a useful addition to sauces, jams and desserts, as well as making an attractive garnish. Like all citrus fruits, lemons are high in Vitamin C.

¾ *cup castor sugar*
1 *tablespoon butter, melted*
2 *tablespoons self-raising flour*
2 *lemons*
2 *eggs, separated*
⅔ *cup milk*
1 *tablespoon toasted desiccated coconut*

METHOD

1. Mix sugar and butter together in a large microware container.
2. Stir in flour, the grated rind of 1 lemon and juice of both, egg yolks and milk.
3. Beat egg whites until stiff. Fold through mixture. Sprinkle with coconut.
4. Cook, elevated on a roasting rack off the centre of the turntable, on MEDIUM-HIGH (70–80%) for 7 minutes, moving the dish from one side of the turntable to the other half-way through cooking time.
5. Stand for 1 minute. Serve with whipped cream.

VARIATIONS

- Add 1 tablespoon desiccated coconut with flour.
- Use oranges or limes instead of lemons.

SERVES 4

PREPARATION TIME
5 minutes

COOKING TIME
8 minutes

UTENSILS
Large container (1.5 litre)
Roasting rack

EASY TIPS
Citrus fruits will yield more juice if warmed in the microwave for 30–40 seconds on HIGH (90–100%) before squeezing.

To toast coconut, scatter 100 g on a microwave-safe plate and cook on HIGH (90–100%) for 4–6 minutes. Stir several times during cooking to ensure it does not burn.

BAKED APPLES

SERVES 4

PREPARATION TIME
5 minutes

COOKING TIME
7 minutes

UTENSIL
Medium container (1 litre)

ACCESSORY
Paper towel

Apples are Australia's second favourite fruit, after oranges, and are low in kilojoules whilst supplying a range of vitamins and minerals. They make a delicious dessert, as microwave cooking highlights their refreshing flavour and colour.

4 Granny Smith apples, cored
⅓ cup sultanas
1 tablespoon brown sugar
2 tablespoons rolled oats
1 lemon

METHOD
1. Pierce skins of apples and place around edge of medium microware container.
2. Mix sultanas, sugar, oats, grated rind of lemon and 1 tablespoon lemon juice together. Fill core cavity with fruit mixture.
3. Cover with paper towel. Cook on HIGH (90–100%) for 5–6 minutes. Pour juices over apple. Stand 1½ minutes and then serve.

VARIATION
• Use chopped dried apricots and sherry in the filling.

SERVING SUGGESTION
• Serve with Custard (see page 115) or cream.

EASY TIP
Rearrange baked apples during cooking for even results. Turn each fruit so the outside edge moves to the inside of container.

TWO-FRUIT CRUMBLE

There's a huge saving in time and electricity costs when cooking desserts in the microwave oven and, as a bonus, your kitchen remains cool in hot weather.

1 × 425 g can pie apple
1 × 425 g can pie apricots
⅓ cup self-raising flour
40 g butter, chilled
3 tablespoons brown sugar
3 tablespoons toasted coconut
⅓ cup toasted rolled oats

METHOD
❶ Mix apple and apricot together in a large microware container.
❷ Rub butter into flour to resemble breadcrumbs. Add sugar, coconut and oats. Mix well. Sprinkle evenly over fruit in container.
❸ Cook, uncovered, on HIGH (90–100%) for 10 minutes off the centre of the turntable, moving the dish from one side of the turntable to the other half-way through cooking. Stand 3 minutes before serving.

VARIATION
● Use ½ cup toasted muesli instead of coconut and oats.

SERVING SUGGESTION
● Serve with Custard (see page 115), cream or ice-cream.

SERVES 4

PREPARATION TIME
10 minutes

COOKING TIME
13 minutes

UTENSIL
Large container (1.5 litre)

EASY TIPS
Fruit crumble can be placed under a hot grill to crispen topping if cooked in an ovenable glass dish.

Cook 500 g of peeled, cored and sliced apple in a covered microware container on HIGH (90–100%) for 5 minutes for freshly stewed fruit.

BAKED LEMON CHEESECAKE

SERVES 6

PREPARATION TIME
10 minutes

COOKING TIME
17 minutes

UTENSILS
20 cm ovenable round glass pie dish
Roasting rack

Cheesecake is always popular with Australians as a dessert and cooked in the microwave it is much easier and takes just a third of the time of conventionally baked cheesecake. The texture is creamy and it tastes delicious. For convenience, serve this cake straight from the pie dish.

50 g butter, melted
1 cup crushed butternut snap biscuits
250 g cream cheese
250 g ricotta cheese
⅓ cup sugar
2 lemons
2 eggs

METHOD
1 Melt butter in a 20 cm round ovenable glass pie dish on HIGH (90–100%) for 45 seconds.
2 Add biscuit crumbs and mix thoroughly. Press evenly over the base and up the sides of dish.
3 Roughly chop cream cheese into a bowl or jug and soften on MEDIUM (50–60%) for 1 minute. Beat until smooth.
4 Add ricotta, sugar, grated rind and juice of lemons and eggs. Beat together well.
5 Pour into prepared pie dish. Cook, elevated on a roasting rack, on MEDIUM (50–60%) for 15 minutes.
6 Stand on bench to set. When cool chill in refrigerator.

EASY TIP
To remove cheesecake from an ovenable glass pie plate, line the dish with plastic wrap, ensuring that 4 cm hangs over the edges of the dish, before pressing crumbs onto the wrap. Prepare the cake as directed.

VARIATIONS
● Use honeysnap, gingernut, marie or chocolate ripple biscuits for the base.
● Add ½ cup chocolate chips to mixture.

TOASTED HONEY BREAD AND BUTTER PUDDING

Old-fashioned bread pudding makes a perfect finishing touch to any meal. Using raisin bread saves time, and lightly toasted bread adds colour and crunch to the recipe.

4 slices fruit loaf bread, toasted and lightly
  buttered
3 × 61 g eggs at room temperature
1 cup milk, at room temperature
¼ cup honey

SERVES 4

PREPARATION TIME
8 minutes

COOKING TIME
7 minutes

UTENSIL
Large container (1.5 litre)

METHOD

❶ Cut buttered toast into triangles and arrange around edge of large microware container.
❷ Mix eggs, milk and honey together thoroughly. Pour over toast.
❸ Cover. Place container on the edge of turntable. Cook on HIGH (90–100%) for 5 minutes, moving to the opposite side of the turntable half-way through cooking.
❹ Stand for 2 minutes.

VARIATION
● Sprinkle with toasted nuts or include a layer of drained canned fruit.

SERVING SUGGESTION
● Serve with cream or ice-cream.

EASY TIPS
For easy pouring, remove metal lid and soften honey in its jar for 15 seconds on HIGH (90–100%).

For perfect custard results, ensure all the ingredients are at room temperature before cooking.

CHOCOLATE CONES

SERVES 4

PREPARATION TIME
4 minutes

COOKING TIME
2 minutes

UTENSIL
Ovenable glass jug

ACCESSORY
Baking paper

EASY TIPS
Milk, dark or white chocolate can be used for cones.

If using chocolate buttons, there is no need to chop them. They speed cooking time also as small pieces of chocolate melt more quickly than large.

Never cover chocolate when melting.

Chocolate doesn't become runny when melted in the microwave. It retains its shape but the appearance changes from dull to glossy. It should then be stirred.

Chocolate is always a winner and these filled cones will make any entertaining a special occasion. Use compounded chocolate as it sets firmly at room temperature. Cooking chocolate will not hold its shape.

150 g compounded chocolate
2 tablespoons chocolate hazelnut spread
½ cup thickened cream, lightly whipped

METHOD
1 Chop chocolate into squares. Place in an ovenable glass jug. Melt on MEDIUM-HIGH (70–80%) for approximately 2 minutes, stirring occasionally.
2 Cut baking paper into two 10 cm squares. Cut each diagonally to make four triangles. Fold each triangle into a cone-shape and secure with sticky tape.
3 Brush the inside of each cone with a layer of chocolate, taking care to keep shape. Allow chocolate to set and then fill cones with a layer of chocolate hazelnut spread and top with cream.
4 Remove paper to serve.

VARIATIONS
● Fill cones with a fruit purée mixed with whipped cream.
● Fill cones with ice-cream.
● Instead of rolling paper into cones, cut into circles and drape over the base of a glass to make cups.

SERVING SUGGESTION
● Serve with fresh fruit and whipped cream.

INDIVIDUAL STEAMED PUDDINGS

Individual puddings cook in mere minutes in the microwave, making an ideal winter dessert that also looks special when entertaining. Cooking individual desserts allows the flavour to be easily altered to suit each person.

2 tablespoons jam
80 g butter
⅓ cup castor sugar
1 egg, lightly beaten
¼ cup milk
¾ cup self-raising flour

METHOD

1 Spread a quarter of the jam over base of each ovenable glass bowl.

2 Melt butter in ovenable glass jug on HIGH (90–100%) for 40 seconds.

3 Add sugar and stir well. Add egg and milk, then flour. Stir with a fork until well combined.

4 Spoon into individual glass bowls to half fill. Cover with plastic wrap and place on outer edge of the turntable.

5 Cook on HIGH (90–100%) for 2½ minutes.

6 Stand puddings for 1 minute before running a knife around the edge and unmolding into serving dishes.

VARIATIONS

● Use golden syrup instead of jam.
● Add 1 tablespoon cocoa with sugar and serve with chocolate sauce.

SERVING SUGGESTION

● Serve with Custard (see page 115), cream or ice-cream.

SERVES 4

PREPARATION TIME
8 minutes

COOKING TIME
4–5 minutes

UTENSILS
1 litre ovenable glass jug
4 × 1 cup ovenable glass bowls

ACCESSORY
Plastic wrap

EASY TIPS
Glass bowls produce a good steamed texture and are easy to unmould.

Tea cups can be substituted for bowls.

SAUCES

A simple home-made sauce can make all the difference to an everyday meal. Sauces cook evenly in the microwave oven, liberating the cook from continual stirring. Microwave sauces do not become lumpy, stick to the pan or burn.

- Use an ovenable glass jug of the right size to make sauces in. You can measure, mix and cook in the jug, and the handle will remain cool.
- A larger jug than normal is used for milk-based sauces, to prevent boil overs.
- The absence of direct heat in the microwave oven means that less fluid is needed as sauces do not reduce as much as with stove-top cooking.
- If ingredients for a sauce have come straight from the refrigerator the cooking time will be a little longer.
- Use paper towel as a cover if constant stirring is required.
- Stir occasionally to prevent overcooking near the outer surfaces – stirring will ensure that your sauce is smooth and evenly textured.
- Make sure you boil flour- or cornflour-based sauces so they thicken. Do not boil egg-yolk sauces or they may curdle.
- Do not panic if your white sauce is a blob, as it can be put in a blender or processor briefly to smoothen.
- Thin sauces that have become too thick with water, stock or wine rather than milk and stir well before reheating.

WHITE SAUCE

When sauces have all surfaces exposed to microwaves, they cook evenly, eliminating the problems of lumping, sticking and scorching. Use an ovenable glass jug for cooking and stirring convenience.

25 g butter
2 tablespoons flour
1 cup milk, at room temperature
salt and pepper to taste

METHOD

❶ Place butter in an ovenable glass jug and melt on HIGH (90–100%) for 30 seconds.
❷ Add flour, stir well. Cook on HIGH (90–100%) for 1 minute.
❸ Add a third of the milk and stir well to dissolve. Blend in remaining milk.
❹ Cook on HIGH (90–100%) for 2½–3 minutes, stirring regularly until thickened. Season to taste. Stand 1 minute.

VARIATIONS

● For a thinner, pouring sauce use 1½ cups milk.
● Use evaporated milk to make a richer sauce.
● To make cheese sauce, add ½–1 cup grated cheddar cheese and stir to melt.

SERVING SUGGESTIONS

● Use this sauce for Easy Macaroni Cheese (see page 63) or Pumpkin Lasagne (see page 66).
● Pour over Vegetable Medley (see page 78).
● Serve with cauliflower or broccoli.
● Pour over chicken or fish, seasoned with some fresh herbs.

MAKES ABOUT 1 CUP

PREPARATION TIME
2 minutes

COOKING TIME
6 minutes

UTENSIL
500 ml ovenable glass jug

EASY TIP
A microwave spoonwhisk is a great special utensil for sauce-making as it separates the flour particles much more efficiently than a spoon.

TOMATO SAUCE

MAKES 400 ML

PREPARATION TIME
5 minutes

COOKING TIME
14 minutes

UTENSIL
1 litre ovenable glass jug

ACCESSORY
Plastic wrap

Based on a can of tomatoes, this is a quick and delicious sauce to make. I have recommended the use of an ovenable glass jug as the most convenient utensil for sauces as the handle remains cool, making it easy to stir.

1 large onion, chopped
1 × 440 can tomatoes (or 500 g fresh tomatoes, skinned – see page 64)
1 tablespoon tomato paste
1 teaspoon brown sugar
1 tablespoon chopped fresh basil

METHOD
1. Place onion in an ovenable glass jug, cover with plastic wrap and cook on HIGH (90–100%) for 1 minute.
2. Roughly chop tomatoes and add to onion. Stir in tomato paste, sugar and basil. Cover with plastic wrap and cook on HIGH (90–100%) for 10 minutes, stirring once. Stand 3 minutes.
3. Purée all ingredients together. Season to taste.
4. Serve hot or cold.

VARIATION
● Add 250 g browned mince meat (see page 49) and 2 cloves crushed garlic with tomatoes to make a quick Bolognese sauce.

SERVING SUGGESTIONS
● Serve on schnitzel, fish or chicken breasts.
● Use on beef, pork or lamb when you barbecue or cook on a grill.

EASY TIP
If at any time you need fresh basil but only have dried, place 3 tablespoons in 500 ml ovenable glass jug. Add ¼ cup water. Cover the jug with vented plastic wrap and cook on HIGH (90–100%) until the water is absorbed and the basil rehydrated and fragrant.

ORIENTAL SAUCE

This aromatic sauce is a good accompaniment to many main dishes. Try it on pork fillets, chicken or fish fillets.

2 tablespoons cornflour
1 tablespoon sugar
1 tablespoon soy sauce
1 tablespoon tomato sauce
1 tablespoon malt vinegar
1 tablespoon dry sherry
⅔ cup orange juice, at room temperature

MAKES 300 ML

PREPARATION TIME
3 minutes

COOKING TIME
3½ minutes

UTENSIL
500 ml ovenable glass jug

METHOD
1 Blend cornflour, sugar, soy sauce, tomato sauce, vinegar and sherry together in an ovenable glass jug. Then stir in orange juice.
2 Cook on HIGH (90–100%) for 2½ minutes, stirring regularly until thickened. Stand 45 seconds.

VARIATIONS
- Add some ground ginger or Chinese five-spice with the cornflour.
- Add some chopped spring onions to garnish.

SERVING SUGGESTION
- Serve over chicken and pork fillets or meatballs.

EASY TIPS
Fresh, room temperature orange juice has been used. If using packaged chilled juice, sauce will take approximately 1 minute longer to cook.

Oranges will yield more juice if warmed in the microwave for 30–40 seconds on HIGH (90–100%) before squeezing.

GRAVY

A good gravy is the making of many a meal, especially roast dinners. Classic sauces are simple to make in the microwave.

1 tablespoon gravy flour or cornflour
1 cup hot tap water
1 beef stock cube

METHOD

① Mix gravy flour with a little cold water to a smooth paste.
② Crumble stock cube into 1 cup hot water in an ovenable glass jug. Cook on HIGH (90–100%) for 1 minute.
③ Stir into flour paste thoroughly. Cook on HIGH (90–100%) for one minute, stirring very well every 20 seconds until thickened.

VARIATIONS

● Use strong beef stock instead of water and stock cube.
● Use ½ teaspoon Vegemite and ¼ teaspoon Worcestershire sauce instead of stock cube, for flavour and colour.

SERVING SUGGESTION

● Serve over roast meats, poultry or meatloaf.

EASY TIPS
Make up cup hot water with meat juices from roasts.

During cooking, regular whisking keeps the gravy smooth and ensures more even cooking.

INSTANT HOLLANDAISE SAUCE

The microwave is the easiest way to make this delicious but tricky and delicate sauce that can separate. Using a low power prevents boiling, which results in curdling.

1 tablespoon butter
1 egg yolk, beaten
1 teaspoon lemon juice
salt and pepper
dash of paprika (optional)
2 tablespoons yoghurt (optional)

METHOD

❶ Place butter in ovenable glass jug and microwave on HIGH (90–100%) for 20–30 seconds until melted but not greasy.
❷ Blend in egg, lemon juice, salt, pepper and paprika.
❸ Microwave on LOW (30–40%) for 30–40 seconds, stirring every 15 seconds until thick. Do not overcook as sauce will curdle.
❹ Stir in yoghurt until smooth, if desired.

VARIATION

● Use orange juice instead of lemon juice and add some orange zest if serving with fish such as trout.

SERVING SUGGESTION

● Serve with fish or lightly cooked vegetables.

SERVES 2

PREPARATION TIME
2 minutes

COOKING TIME
1 minute

UTENSIL
250 ml ovenable glass jug

EASY TIPS
If mixture separates, whip vigorously until smooth.

Mock hollandaise can be made by adding 2 beaten egg yolks, 1 tablespoon lemon juice and 1 tablespoon butter to a medium white sauce. Heat through on MEDIUM-HIGH *(70–80%) for 1 minute to blend.*

SATAY SAUCE

MAKES 1 CUP

PREPARATION TIME
5 minutes

COOKING TIME
4 minutes

UTENSIL
500 ml ovenable glass jug

A piquant dipping sauce that's great for chicken, meat or fish.

1 small onion, finely chopped
1 clove garlic, crushed
⅓ cup peanut butter
1 tablespoon soy sauce
2 tablespoons vinegar or lemon juice
⅓ cup water
½–1 teaspoon chilli sauce

METHOD

❶ Place onion and garlic in ovenable glass jug. Cook on HIGH (90–100%) for 1 minute.

❷ Add remaining ingredients and stir well. Cook on HIGH (90–100%) for 2 minutes, stirring once during cooking. Stand 1 minute.

SERVING SUGGESTIONS

● Serve over beef, chicken or fish kebabs as a sauce.

● Use sauce as a marinade for meat, then cook in sauce.

EASY TIP
To make peanut butter spreadable, remove the metal lid and microwave the jar on HIGH (90–100%) *for 30–60 seconds and stir.*

HANDY CHOCOLATE SAUCE

Keep a quantity of this handy chocolate sauce in the fridge as it reheats well on MEDIUM (50–60%). Serve over desserts, puddings or poached fruit.

3 tablespoons cocoa
4 tablespoons sugar
1 tablespoon cornflour
1 cup milk, at room temperature
50 g butter, chopped
1 teaspoon vanilla essence

METHOD

❶ Blend cocoa, sugar and cornflour together with a third of the milk in ovenable glass jug until lump free.

❷ Add remaining milk. Cook on HIGH (90–100%) for 3 minutes, stirring well each minute.

❸ Add butter and vanilla and stir until melted and smooth.

❹ Serve warm or pour into a jar and store in the refrigerator.

VARIATIONS

● Add ¼ teaspoon ground cinnamon to cocoa.

● Add 2 tablespoons alcohol (e.g. brandy, Grand Marnier) with butter for extra flavour.

● For a richer sauce, use cream instead of milk.

SERVING SUGGESTIONS

● Serve warm over steamed puddings or fudge as a dessert.

● Serve cold over ice-cream, poached pears or as a filling for meringues.

MAKES ABOUT
300 ML

PREPARATION TIME
5 minutes

COOKING TIME
4 minutes

UTENSIL
500 ml ovenable glass jug

EASY TIP
When cooling, cover sauce with plastic wrap to prevent skin forming.

CUSTARD

Custard cooked in the microwave does not stick or become lumpy. Stirring is minimal and the clean-up is easy.

2 tablespoons custard powder
1 tablespoon castor sugar
1½ cups milk, at room temperature
1 teaspoon vanilla essence (optional)

METHOD

❶ Mix custard powder and sugar with a little milk in a jug until a smooth, lump-free paste. Add remaining milk and vanilla.

❷ Cook on HIGH (90–100%) for 2 minutes. Stir and cook another 2 minutes, stirring every 30 seconds. Stand 1 minute.

VARIATIONS

● Add 1 sliced banana to cooked custard.
● Extra milk can be added for a thinner, pouring custard.

SERVING SUGGESTIONS

● Serve over desserts.
● Use cold in trifle.

SERVES 4

PREPARATION TIME
2 minutes

COOKING TIME
5 minutes

UTENSIL
1 litre ovenable glass jug

EASY TIPS
To turn into an egg custard, whisk in an egg at the end of cooking time. It will cook in the heat of the custard as it stands.

Covering custard with plastic wrap during standing time prevents a skin forming.

JAMS AND CHUTNEY

Jams and chutneys are best made with the 'cook and stir' microwave method, and for maximum freshness in small quantities. They can be kept in the refrigerator, or given as a special gift.

- Cook small quantities using fresh, good quality fruit. Don't try to cook more than 2 cups berries, 1 kg stone fruit or 3 citrus fruits for marmalade at one time.
- Use commercial pectin, especially with moist berries – proportions are about the same proportion of ingredients as in cooking conventionally.
- Place absorbent paper towel under the cooking container for an easy clean-up if jam boils over.
- Stir to distribute the heat and blend ingredients.
- Sterilise glass bottles or jars in the microwave.
- Check the setting point of jam by pouring a little onto a cold saucer. Place in the refrigerator for 2 minutes. If a skin forms on top that wrinkles when pushed with a finger setting point has been reached.

Always use the right size and shape container as these affect cooking results.

ANY FRUIT JAM

**MAKES ABOUT 3–4 ×
300 ML JARS**

PREPARATION TIME
2 minutes

COOKING TIME
15 minutes

UTENSIL
*Extra-large microwave
container (2.25 litres)*

This jam can be made of any fresh fruit.
Stone or pip fruit where necessary.

*1 kg stoned fruit, washed
1 kg castor sugar
Jamsetta*

METHOD
1. Place fruit in bowl. Cover and cook on
   HIGH (90–100%) for 5 minutes.
2. Add sugar. Stir to dissolve and cook,
   uncovered, on HIGH (90–100%) for another
   5 minutes, stirring half-way through
   cooking time.
3. Add ½ packet Jamsetta for strawberries,
   ⅓ packet for any other fruit. Cook a
   further 5 minutes on HIGH (90–100%).
4. Let cool a little then pour into sterilised
   glass jars and seal.

SERVING SUGGESTION
● Use in trifle.

EASY TIP
*To sterilise jam jars in the
microwave: place 2–3 cm
boiled water in clean glass
jars; cook, uncovered, on
HIGH (90–100%) until water
boils; remove jars from
oven, put tops on and
leave while making jam.
Empty water out when
you are ready to fill jars.*

ALL SEASONS JAM

Jam made in the microwave has lively, freshly picked colour. For a good shelf life, jams must be stored in sterilised containers.

500 g dried apricots
2 cups hot water
1 cup sugar
2 tablespoons lemon juice

METHOD
❶ Place apricots and water in ovenable glass jug. Cook on HIGH (90–100%) for 15 minutes.
❷ Add sugar and stir through well to dissolve. Cook on HIGH (90–100%) for 10 minutes, stirring once half-way through cooking time.
❸ Stir well to break up apricots. Mix in lemon juice.
❹ Spoon into sterilised glass jars and seal.

VARIATION
● Any dried fruit may be used, or a mixture, e.g. apple and apricot.

SERVING SUGGESTION
● Spread on toast, scones or plain damper.

**MAKES ABOUT 3 ×
300 ML JARS**

PREPARATION TIME
2 minutes

COOKING TIME
25 minutes

UTENSIL
1 litre ovenable glass jug

EASY TIPS
Plumping up apricot halves is faster than rehydrating whole fruit.

To sterilise jam jars in the microwave: place 2–3 cm boiled water in clean glass jars; cook, uncovered, on HIGH (90–100%) until water boils; remove jars from oven, put tops on and leave while making jam. Empty water out when you are ready to fill jars.

FRUIT CHUTNEY

**MAKES ABOUT 2 ×
300 ML JARS**

PREPARATION TIME
10 minutes

COOKING TIME
1 hour

UTENSIL
1 litre ovenable glass jug

A chunky, spicy fruit preserve made easily in the microwave.

4 large Granny Smith apples
4 large onions
½ cup currants
10 cloves
1½ cups cider vinegar
1 cup brown sugar

METHOD

1. Peel and core apples. Dice apples and onion and place in jug with remaining ingredients.
2. Cover, cook on HIGH (90–100%) for 15 minutes until boiling.
3. Stir well. Cook, uncovered, on HIGH (90–100%) for 40–45 minutes, stirring 2–3 times until thick.
4. Pour into sterilised jars and seal.

VARIATIONS

- Use sultanas instead of currants.
- Add 2 mashed bananas with apple.
- Add 1 teaspoon mustard seeds.

SERVING SUGGESTIONS

- Serve with roast meats or spread on sandwiches.
- Use to enhance flavour in other sauces.
- Glaze meatloaf with it, and serve as accompanying sauce.

Index

....